T0356373

"*The DBT Workbook to Stop Walking on Eggshells* provides an accessible, practical guide to navigating the complexities of high-stress relationships with wisdom and empathy. Through clear, actionable dialectical behavior therapy (DBT) skills, the authors offer strategies to build emotional resilience and establish healthier boundaries. This workbook is a great tool for anyone looking to manage relational challenges while cultivating personal peace and more meaningful connections."

> —**Marcus Rodriguez, PhD**, associate professor at Pitzer College, and director of the Youth and Family Institute in Los Angeles, CA

"This book is an excellent resource for families and professionals alike. Written with deep knowledge of the complex and sometimes confusing mental health condition, borderline personality disorder (BPD), it provides a clear path to improved family relationships. Based on many years of experience working with families of individuals with BPD, it brings compassion, kindness, and wisdom to all involved without compromising fidelity to DBT principles. Highly recommended."

> —**Tania Alexander**, clinical psychologist, and director of the DBT Psychology Clinic in Sydney, Australia

"This user-friendly guide empowers families and friends to understand and more effectively connect with emotionally volatile loved ones. Clear explanations, engaging exercises, and relatable examples teach essential skills to help readers and those they care about manage emotionally turbulent interactions. It is so wonderful to have this new workbook that translates the invaluable benefits inspired by DBT into easy-to-apply strategies. Highly recommended!"

> —**Ronda Oswalt Reitz, PhD**, DBT trainer, consultant, and therapist

"Learning and practicing the skills so aptly explained in *The DBT Workbook to Stop Walking on Eggshells* has radically changed my relationship with our daughter with BPD. I had lost all hope, and now I am able to embrace our relationship with gratitude and relief. The authors' tender and thoughtful communication about this painful subject has truly rescued our family from despair in a way I never thought possible."

> —**Marcy**, mother of a teenage daughter with BPD

"If you want to get off the hamster wheel of high emotions, conflict, pain, and exhaustion with your loved one, and help yourself and the person with BPD traits, please find the time to go through this workbook carefully and consistently. The skills outlined in this workbook changed the trajectory of my daughter's dysregulation so much that she no longer fulfills the criteria for BPD."

—**Angie**, mother of an adult daughter with BPD

"The tools in this workbook will give you the skills you need to navigate difficult relationships with highly sensitive loved ones, whether they are diagnosed with BPD or not. You will improve your ability to accept your loved ones for who they are, communicate with them, stop reinforcing negative behaviors, forgive your own mistakes, and ultimately get more out of your relationships. You will find yourself referring to these tools over and over again."

—**W. D.**, partner of a loved one with symptoms of BPD

"When my daughter's therapist diagnosed her with BPD, many things finally made sense, yet I couldn't quite grasp the challenge we were facing. Our communication was getting worse, and I was frightened for her life. I was feeling as if I had been blindfolded, hands tied behind my back, and recklessly abandoned into a maze. Nowadays, my daughter and I practice the skills in this workbook. It is an amazing compass for keeping my North in sight and not getting lost in such a dysregulated emotional labyrinth

—**Beatriz**, mother of an adult daughter with BPD

"This standout DBT workbook builds on the amazing work of Marsha Linehan in this area. Real-life examples put key DBT concepts into context. The practical exercises help the reader identify ways to use the skills in their own situation. This book transformed my family's life. Our reward has been a dramatic improvement in our relationship with our son who struggles with extreme emotions. We anticipate similar relationship improvements with our adult BPD loved ones."

—**William**, father of two adults and a teenage son with BPD

The

DBT WORKBOOK

to stop

walking on

eggshells

**Practical Skills for Families to
Improve Relationships & Decrease Conflict
When a Family Member Has BPD**

Corrine Stoewsand, PhD
Randi Kreger | Carola Pechon

New Harbinger Publications, Inc.

Publisher's Note

This publication is designed to provide accurate and authoritative information in regard to the subject matter covered. It is sold with the understanding that the publisher is not engaged in rendering psychological, financial, legal, or other professional services. If expert assistance or counseling is needed, the services of a competent professional should be sought.

NEW HARBINGER PUBLICATIONS is a registered trademark of New Harbinger Publications, Inc.

New Harbinger Publications is an employee-owned company.

Copyright © 2025 by Corrine Stoewsand, Randi Kreger, and Carola Pechon
New Harbinger Publications, Inc.
5720 Shattuck Avenue
Oakland, CA 94609
www.newharbinger.com

All Rights Reserved

Cover design by Amy Shoup

Illustrations by Jodi Rector-Brooks

Acquired by Georgia Kolias

Edited by Jennifer Holder

Library of Congress Cataloging-in-Publication Data on file

Printed in the United States of America

27   26   25

10   9   8   7   6   5   4   3   2   1   First Printing

Contents

Foreword

If you have been told, or have come to believe, that there is nothing you can do when faced with a family member who suffers from intense emotional suffering, please know that this book has been written to shatter that notion!

Because you are reading this book, it's likely that you are very concerned about a loved one. Perhaps you have run the gamut of emotions such as anger, sadness, disappointment, and fear that might sometimes be experienced as terror. You may have intense confusion about why it is that the things that seemed to work for you in life are failing in your interactions with this person. Your loved one may engage in behaviors that put them at grave risk, and you feel at an utter loss to help them.

While it's important to acknowledge there is much in life that we don't have control over, it is important to recognize where we can have an impact. I have often heard the saying, "It takes two to tango." While some use this phrase as a way to blame others for their contributions to problems in relationships, it really acknowledges that all relationships are influenced and changed by both people in them, for better and worse, whether we are aware of it or not. This book focuses on how to become aware of your influence on relationships and act in skillful ways that foster positive change. At the same time, I don't want to minimize the difficulties you are facing or create the impression this is easy. So, in true DBT (dialectical behavior therapy) fashion, the book also provides the tools needed to tolerate situations when they don't go as you would like.

I had the good fortune of meeting Corrine Stoewsand, the lead author of this book, in 2014 when she was living in Buenos Aires and working with Fundación Foro, an organization dedicated to providing the most effective treatment to people with the most difficult to treat mental health problems. Her strong intellect and steadfast practice in mindfulness join with her values of compassion, service, and science to help family members of those who so often don't know where to turn.

This book offers a set of skills tested in research centers in multiple countries to help those who experience such suffering that they are at risk for suicide. Many years ago, it was observed and studied that these skills can also be helpful to patients' families, social support networks, and treatment providers. This book can potentially close a significant gap by offering the help family members need.

Early in my career as a mental health professional, I was advised to never treat people with borderline personality disorder (BPD), the diagnosis most associated with emotional suffering and suicide risk, because they were believed to be untreatable. We now live in a time when no one aware of developments in mental health treatments can make such a claim. Today, I can say that I have been fortunate to know many people who have either overcome BPD or have successfully managed living with it. There are clearly ways to skillfully address problems related to intense emotional suffering while accepting what it means to live with emotional sensitivity. If you or your loved ones experience a high level of emotional sensitivity, I underscore that with all the difficulties this may present you, sensitivity can also be a personal strength. Some of the greatest artists, thinkers, and therapists have such experiences!

Dr. Marsha Linehan, the developer of DBT, has always been clear that her mission is to get those who suffer "out of hell." This mission developed from her own extreme difficulties in her teenage years. She has been steadfast that if she could get out of hell, so can you. Please take this to heart! I am most grateful to these authors for writing this book as another means of helping people get out of hell. I want to extend great hope to those of you who read it, that you can find and create a life that meets the goals and values dearest to your hearts, and that you can experience healing and fulfillment in your relationships with your loved ones.

—Anthony P. DuBose, PsyD
Vice President for Institute Services,
Behavioral Tech Institute, Seattle, WA

Introduction

Managing a loving relationship with someone who is emotionally sensitive, insecure, and reactive can be challenging. If you know or suspect they have borderline personality disorder (BPD), you may feel even more scared and desperate for guidance. Your friends and relatives don't understand, give you bad advice, and might even blame you for the problem—all while you are trapped in endless pain, confusion, and misery.

If you really want to get out of this hell, dialectical behavior therapy (DBT) skills can be transformative. You can reduce your pain and confusion while increasing your understanding and clarity. You can learn how to respond far more effectively to your sensitive loved one, reduce conflict, and improve communication. DBT skills and principles can guide your interactions with everyone in your life—not only a difficult loved one.

This book offers a complete program to help you understand emotional dysregulation and learn essential DBT skills to change yourself and your relationship with your loved one. Step by step, the skills will help you:

1. Practice and develop skills to improve your well-being and gain emotional balance for yourself.

2. Focus on changing your behavior using skills to reduce your stress, improve emotional balance, communicate effectively, and feel more connected. (You will also model this new, more effective behavior to others.)

3. Apply these skills to a difficult relationship. More skillful communication and behavior will activate fewer emotional reactions and crises. If they do occur, you will be able to respond more effectively.

4. Share these skills by practicing together.

5. Teach or explain a skill you use and how it helps you.

Of course, not everyone gets to step four or five. This is a gentle guide along a path that first focuses on you and your well-being, helps you apply skills to improve a difficult relationship, and may help your loved one improve their well-being.

Maybe you just want to get your loved one into therapy. Be patient! Your loved one did not begin having emotional and interpersonal challenges yesterday, and they will not be solved tomorrow. Do not push your loved one "kicking and screaming" into therapy. It's unlikely to be effective. Let go and do your own work. Clean up "your side of the street" in the relationship, which is all you can really do anyway.

Research shows that 86 percent of the outcomes of mental health treatments result from factors outside therapy, in the places where a person lives and works (Wampold and Imel 2015). In other words, relationships with family, friends, and coworkers can have more powerful influences on mental health than a therapist. Please remember that while learning these skills and attending to your emotional health!

DBT is the most widely researched treatment for borderline personality disorder. Few therapists are trained in helping families navigate a relationship with a loved one with BPD. We do not expect you to become a family member's therapist. Instead, you can respond in a way that is more likely to improve your whole family's well-being.

What Is BPD?

Borderline personality disorder is one of ten personality disorders, according to the American Psychiatric Association. BPD is characterized by intense emotional reactivity and significant interpersonal instability. BPD is marked by chronic hypervigilance about being rejected or put down, sometimes labeled "fear of abandonment"; impulsivity sometimes to the point of self-harm; and feelings of emptiness. In severe cases or under stress, paranoia and dissociation also occur.

A person with BPD may have a confused sense of self—they may not feel able to direct their own goals and behavior, so they often scan the environment for what to think, feel, or do. Someone suffering from BPD may experience other people and the external environment as the source of their problems and suffering; therefore, they cannot be expected to be responsible for their actions or direct their behavior appropriately.

BPD is associated with problems in interpersonal functioning. *Empathy,* the ability to understand the inner experience and motivations of others, is compromised by expectations of being slighted or put down, sensitivity to other's negative motivations and bad intentions, and feeling overwhelmed upon observing emotional distress in others. Intimacy is often marked by mistrust, neediness, worry about rejection, and alternation between overinvolvement and withdrawal. Interpersonal relationships may be highly conflictive or unstable (American Psychiatric Association 2016).

These impairments are usually intermittent. They increase during periods of stress and emotional dysregulation. They decrease when your loved one feels safe and calm.

---

exercise: Observing Your Loved One

Read the following questions. If your response is "yes," reflect on when you observed the behavior and describe at least one example.

Have you observed that your loved one can be deeply insecure and ashamed despite expressing rage, contempt, or perfectionism?

_____

_____

_____

_____

Has your loved one doubted their perception, capacities, or decisions—or spoken in excessively self-critical terms?

_____

_____

_____

_____

_____

Has your loved one denied responsibility for their actions or blamed others for their behavior?

_____

_____

_____

_____

_____

Can you think of an example of when your loved one seemed lacking in empathy or was blind to another's feelings?

_____

_____

_____

_____

_____

Do they sometimes appear hyper-empathic or anxious to relieve another's distress?

_____

_____

_____

_____

_____

Can you remember an incident when your loved one tried to avoid, attack, or push others away when what they really seemed to want was connection and belonging more than anything else?

_____

_____

_____

_____

_____

Just because you understand a little about BPD, don't start reporting your diagnosis to your loved one! Telling someone they have a "disordered personality" can be derogatory and judgmental. Some people react explosively. Some might be curious and open to see if the description resonates. In any case, knowing or even agreeing with the diagnosis does not magically make it go away.

It's more effective to follow all instructions in this workbook. Develop and practice all the skills to improve communication, reinforce positive behavior, and, when the time is right or when your loved one asks for help, support your loved one to connect with a qualified clinician.

BPD affects between 2.7 and 5.9 percent of the world's population (Grant et al. 2008). Interpersonal difficulties, emotional dysregulation, and sensitivity to criticism or rejections are not exclusive to BPD. There is increasing awareness of misdiagnoses and co-occurrence of BPD with other conditions, making diagnosing even more complicated. However, experiencing intense, painful emotions is not a life sentence. There is real hope for your loved one. Consider the experience of Tita and her daughter, Marsha.

◆ *Tita and Marsha*

Tita was proud to be a Louisiana Cajun, married to a Texas oil man. They had six children, two girls and four boys, and lived in Tulsa, Oklahoma. When her youngest daughter, Marsha, was seventeen, things began to go wrong. Tita sent her to a residential clinic in New England for "tension and social withdrawal."

Tita received letters from her daughter that described how much she hated being in the clinic and how badly they treated her there. She was self-cutting, burning herself with cigarettes, and wanting to die. She begged her mother to bring her home. Tita cried herself to sleep reading those letters. This residential clinic was supposed to be one of the best in the country. Her daughter's treatment included a long list of psychiatric medications, repeated electroshock treatments, and punishments of seclusion for up to three months.

Incredibly, after more than two years of institutional living, Marsha was released without much hope for her survival. In fact, she soon attempted suicide again. And again (Carey 2011). Despite the odds, at twenty-one years old, she started college, studied psychology, and then went on to graduate school. She became a university professor, researcher, and clinical psychologist (Linehan 2020).

Tita's daughter was Marsha Linehan, author and creator of DBT. Dr. Linehan has received numerous scientific awards for contributions to suicidology, clinical psychology, and education. DBT has benefited millions of people around the world. Fifty-four years after being released from that clinic, in 2018, she was named in TIME magazine's special edition on "Great Scientists: The Geniuses and Visionaries Who Transformed Our World."

Imagine how things could have been different if Tita had this workbook. If Tita could have learned and practiced the skills her daughter later developed, she might have understood her daughter better and avoided extreme measures in her desperate attempt to help Marsha.

Marsha Linehan is not the only person who recovered from intense emotional suffering and suicidal behavior. These behaviors are most commonly associated with a BPD diagnosis. Studies have found that 35 percent of people diagnosed with BPD while hospitalized for a psychiatric crisis experienced *diagnostic remission* (no longer met criteria for BPD) within two years. After ten years, 91 percent experienced remission, and after twenty years, 99 percent experienced remission.

"Recovery" of social and occupational functioning goes far beyond remission of symptoms. Long-term studies have shown that 50 percent of people diagnosed and hospitalized for BPD experienced good to excellent recovery within ten years (Zanarini et al. 2018).

How to Use This Workbook

You will not gain better communication and emotional regulation skills just by reading. As you come to each exercise, please stop reading and take time to write down your responses! Practicing and writing are important ways to cultivate emotional balance and plan more effective responses. Also, please download free tools that include worksheets, a resource list, a self-assessment quiz, and a bonus chapter on dialectical communication. Access these at http://www.newharbinger.com/54223 to deepen your knowledge and support your skills practice.

CHAPTER 1

Understanding Emotional Dysregulation

Does your loved one launch a barrage of criticism against you, blame you for all their problems, and then refuse to engage in reciprocal dialogue? Does it seem that anything you say to explain yourself will further escalate their irrational thoughts and behavior? Or perhaps you have been estranged for months or longer from a loved one who you helped and supported for many years.

You're probably looking for a way to get your loved one to calm down and stop reacting, misinterpreting others, and spinning out of control emotionally. You want to figure out how to get this person to take responsibility for their actions. You want to change your loved one's behavior—and it would be for their benefit! Please rest assured: you are not alone.

Emotional Instability in BPD

According to DBT, *emotional dysregulation* is the fundamental characteristic of borderline personality disorder. In fact, in the United Kingdom, BPD is often called emotionally unstable personality disorder. Marsha Linehan compares the level of emotional pain in BPD to someone with third-degree burns all over their body. If you understood how painful it is, you would never poke them. People with BPD may interpret an inconsiderate remark as an intentional poke, then react to the pain as a third-degree emotional burn.

BPD affects thinking and behaving in many complex ways. Many people who suffer from severe emotional dysregulation report feeling "different." Trying to fit in may increase vulnerability and move someone further away from their authentic self, making them feel even more alien. For example, Peter, a twenty-eight-year-old diagnosed with BPD, confided to his brother, David, that "As long as I can remember, I have felt a deep, dark feeling that I don't belong. It's easier to separate myself from others in some way so they won't find out."

Feelings of insecurity go far beyond lack of confidence. Self-criticism, doubt, and a history of insecure connections can sustain intense feelings of worthlessness, even in an accomplished person. Deep and lasting insecurity can be both a cause and an effect of misinterpretations. For example, Cedric told his wife, Serena, "I know everyone in your family hates me. That's why it's so hard to feel good about myself."

BPD is often related to chronic shame, feeling rejected, unloved, and unlovable with an intensity that might bring any of us to our knees in despair. Cheryl often told her mother that she cut herself because "I feel lower than the lowest, most despicable person in the world."

Dialectical behavior therapy (DBT) organizes these seemingly chaotic characteristics of emotional dysregulation into four areas of instability: 1) interpersonal (how one relates to others and communicates with them), 2) cognitive (how one thinks), 3) behavioral (what one says and does), and 4) identity (who one is, what one likes or wants, and how to direct one's actions). The deficiencies in each of these four realms increase with stress and decrease during periods of relative calm.

exercise: Consequences of Emotional Dysregulation

Carefully read the following list of common behaviors and problems. Check any issues that you often observe in your loved one. These are not diagnostic criteria. Your job is *not* to diagnose another person but to understand your loved one's confusing communication and dysfunctional behaviors from a broader perspective. Some are internal experiences, such as thoughts and feelings, and may not necessarily be visible to you.

Interpersonal Instability

The following interpersonal problems are more intense and frequent with intimates and immediate family. In distant relationships, they might not exist at all.

My loved one:

- ☐ Loves me one day and hates me another.

- ☐ Misunderstands the motivations, feelings, beliefs, and experiences of others, especially me.

- ☐ Lacks flexibility in understanding or accepting perspectives, explanations, or memories that differ from their own.

- ☐ Anticipates invalidating responses from others (saying things like "You are going to hate me") and activates self-invalidation (by saying, for example, "I'm a mess").

- ☐ Either relentlessly insists that I immediately fulfill some impulsive desire or is indecisive, unable to state a preference, or alternates between the two.

Cognitive Instability

Many people with personality disorders have plenty of intellect. When anger controls thinking, it might seem like a sharp legal mind emerges to argue relentlessly, but with distorted reasoning and intense demands.

My loved one:

- ☐ Is hypervigilant to being rejected, dismissed, put down, or slighted.

- ☐ Struggles to shift attention away from something distressing or emotionally activating.

- ☐ Can dramatically change seemingly rigidly held opinions and beliefs.

- ☐ Shows signs of emotionally distorted thinking in the moment. For example, their sadness clings to negative memories and ignores the positive. Their anger sees things as unfair. Their fear generates thoughts of threat and danger.

- ☐ Ignores, suppresses, exaggerates, or misinterprets self-needs, feelings, thoughts, and motivations behind their behavior.

Behavioral Instability

Intense emotions drive impulsive urges, automatic reactions, doing or saying things contrary to values, and avoiding social interactions.

My loved one:

- ☐ Has limitations in organizing and coordinating activities independent of mood, including procrastinating, canceling plans, avoiding commitments, and inconsistent attendance at school or work.

- ☐ May give up or act impulsively if they or others do not perform to their standards.

- ☐ Struggles to control impulsive "problem behaviors" (such as self-injury, breaking things, spending money excessively or compulsively, binge eating, vomiting, yelling and insulting, unsafe sex, substance abuse, suicide attempts, hurting others, and more).

- ☐ Habitually avoids, self-isolates, or procrastinates, often due to anxiety and shame.

Identity Instability

Likes and wants are emotionally based, so when your loved one is dysregulated, their sense of self becomes unstable or is pervaded by a sense of emptiness.

My loved one:

- ☐ Feels insecure, inadequate, self-conscious, or worthless.

- ☐ Has difficulty achieving autonomy and independence due to anxiety over decision-making, intolerance of being alone or making a mistake, self-criticism, and inconsistent goals.

- ☐ Is not able to discern what they like or don't like, and has frequently changing interests according to the interests of friends or intimate partners.

- ☐ Makes repeated changes in studies, careers, values, ideals, dreams, and more.

Step back to see how emotional dysregulation is the element underlying what your loved one says and does. This may help you manage your emotional reactions to them and see that it is not personal. Intense emotions repeatedly hijack their thoughts, words, and actions. (Don't let your emotions hijack you by practicing the skills in chapters 2, 3, and 11.)

• *Jill, Brian, and Cheryl*

At twenty-five, Cheryl had been talking about ending her life for more than ten years. Her parents, Jill and Brian, couldn't take it anymore. They decided to stop efforts to convince her that suicide was not the answer. One day, Cheryl said she was researching assisted suicide. Jill responded, "I told you, Cheryl, I don't want to discuss that anymore." Her parents quickly left the house together and drove away.

Cheryl went into an intense rage (emotional instability). She wanted to attack her parents as if that might wake them up and make them want to help her (cognitive instability). She threw stuff around the house and poured cooking oil all over the carpets (behavioral instability). She completely disconnected from her values, lost all sense of herself, and became fused with her anger (identity instability). While the day before she had told them how much she loved them, she wrote "I hate you" on the walls after they left her alone in the house (interpersonal instability).

self-reflection: Your Emotional Dysregulation

To help you understand both your loved one and yourself, consider examples of when *you* became activated in each area (interpersonal, cognitive, behavioral, and identity)—even in small ways. (Did you ever yell at someone or respond with a snarky comment and later regret it?) Even if you only remember one or two items, list them. We all occasionally suffer from intense emotional reactions and impulsive behavior.

_____

_____

_____

_____

_____

_____

_____

_____

_____

The Vicious Cycle

According to DBT's biosocial theory, emotional dysregulation arises from the combination of *emotional vulnerability* and a *chronically invalidating environment*. These biological and social components interact in a vicious circle until a person suffers severe emotional dysregulation. Let's take a look at each component.

Emotional Vulnerability + Chronic Invalidation = Emotional Dysregulation
(biological/physiological)   (environmental/social)

Emotional Vulnerability

An emotional reaction is like a wave. Something activates the emotion; it rises up, reaches a peak, and begins to descend until it has completely passed. Some are more intense and others are very subtle. For people who are sensitive, volatile, or have symptoms of BPD, the emotional profile has the following characteristics:

- **Elevated sensitivity** is characterized by a low threshold at which an emotion is activated and a rapid reaction. A helpful metaphor is a car alarm adjusted to the highest sensitivity to detect motion with zero time delay!

- **Increased intensity** is the tendency to experience more extreme and intense emotions. The metaphorical car alarm is set to maximum volume!

- **Longer duration** of emotion occurs as brain networks are slow to put the brakes on an emotion. Furthermore, the emotion will last longer if the brain cannot redirect attention and thoughts away from the activating event. The timer on the car alarm is set to last longer!

Everyone can experience emotional vulnerability and react with intense emotions that don't resolve quickly. But when a pattern of emotional dysregulation seriously interferes with relationships, communication, and building a life worth living, borderline personality disorder may be involved.

self-reflection: Emotions

Bring to mind a recent time when you felt mild or moderate emotional activation and consider the following questions: Can you remember the "wave"? What did your emotional profile look like? Was it slow or quick to arise? How long was it at its peak? Did you return to baseline quickly and smoothly? Or was it a slower and rockier reduction in intensity before the emotion passed? Describe your experience.

_____

_____

_____

_____

_____

_____

_____

_____

_____

_____

_____

_____

_____

_____

_____

_____

_____

_____

_____

_____

_____

_____

Remember the car alarm, set to detect the tiniest movement and sound off immediately, at the highest volume, for the longest time. Similarly, the central nervous system may be wired to be extremely vulnerable, immediately reactive, leading to intensely painful and longer lasting emotions. These genetic and biological settings may create a predisposition to develop borderline personality disorder. However, not every emotionally sensitive baby develops a personality disorder. With an understanding of emotional vulnerability and the biological basis of BPD, we can move on to consider how chronic invalidation is part of the vicious cycle of emotional dysregulation.

Chronic Invalidation

An invalidating response dismisses, punishes, or trivializes a person's internal experience. Invalidation communicates to a person that their feelings don't matter. Chronic invalidation can lead to insecurity, confusion, and helplessness regarding inner experiences. It can result in an intense dread of possible betrayal, disappointment, or shaming from others. Over time, invalidation installs mistrust of self and others.

Family members often have the best intentions and want to help a loved one who is obviously troubled and suffering. Unfortunately, these good intentions may be invalidating, which only increases emotional dysregulation.

For example, if you say, "Relax, it's no big deal," some people may find that helpful. But if your loved one could just relax, they would. They can't, so these words minimize their experience, which only makes it worse!

Another kind of minimizing is common when family members are frustrated and exhausted. "If she would only get out of bed in the morning" or "If he would just listen to me" are invalidating attitudes and beliefs that can be communicated nonverbally and escalate emotional dysregulation and conflict.

Giving advice or solving someone's problem when they did not ask for help is also invalidating. Unsolicited advice and problem-solving communicate: "I know how to manage your life better than you" or "You don't know what you're doing." You may think you're helping, but your loved one receives underlying messages likely to provoke an even more hurtful emotional reaction.

Validation is not intuitive. It's all too easy to inadvertently invalidate someone's feelings, even when you are trying to help. Later, in chapters 4 and 5, you will learn how to validate. Now, the first and most important step is to stop invalidating your loved one.

• *David and Peter*

David's brother, Peter, was feeling down. He had always been a sensitive guy. His girlfriend of three months had broken up with him. In fact, he was experiencing such sadness that it interfered with his ability to work. Getting up in the morning seemed difficult. He felt exhausted. He could barely function at work. During a telephone conversation with David, Peter told him what was happening.

After patiently listening, David said, "Peter, that relationship only lasted three months. It's not like you were married or anything. And it's affecting your job. Can't you just get up, go to work, and put in a little effort? That's the only way you'll get over this."

David had good intentions. He wanted to help Peter resolve his distress. However, after this conversation, Peter was not just sad and hurt—he felt like a total loser.

self-reflection: Validation

How might David have validated Peter? Try your hand at writing out a more validating response. (*Hint*: *Of course, ending a relationship is painful. Going to work is hard when one feels like s*#!*)

_____

_____

_____

_____

_____

_____

Now, remember David's perspective. How might you validate David? (*Hint*: *Understandably, David might be worried or anxious if Peter has a history of losing jobs.*)

_____

_____

_____

_____

_____

_____

_____

Invalidating Environments

Is your home an invalidating environment? Marsha Linehan describes three types of invalidating families: rigid, chaotic, and normal. Let's examine each.

Rigid Family: In a "rigid" family, everyone is expected to be correct, like the same things, or have the same beliefs and values. They may have high standards for achievement; expectations regarding weight, dress, or physical appearance; or low tolerance for differences in political or religious views.

Chaotic Family: A "chaotic" family has inconsistent and unexpected responses. A child never knows if the parents will be demeaning or proud of them. Parents may respond to their kids based on their own emotional state, without reflecting upon nor understanding the child's inner experience.

Normal Family: The third type of invalidating family is the "normal" family. Parents try to do their best, given all the circumstances. They listen to their kids and ask questions. They try to be patient and empathic most of the time. An emotionally vulnerable child may experience anxiety over the possibility of being slighted in some way. Any correction, minimization, suggestion, constructive criticism, or other slight could be experienced as intensely invalidating. As an adult, there may be memories of being treated unfairly, while all the extras they got as a child are forgotten. Many families have one child who felt invalidated, while none of the siblings felt the same. Unfortunately, babies are not born with a note on their forehead offering information about the sensitivity of their central nervous systems! Even the best parents may unwittingly invalidate their children.

Invalidating environments are not only in homes. Schools, workplaces, social clubs, athletic teams, churches, and any place where people gather can be sources of invalidation. The world is invalidating, as pressure to conform is everywhere. However, invalidation from loved ones and significant others hurts the most.

Of course, the worst invalidation is trauma. Physical or sexual abuse, or a significant traumatic event, can occur anywhere. Traumatic invalidation is a profound message that the world does not care about a person's feelings and their experience does not matter. This can be heartbreaking to family members with a loved one who has experienced such suffering.

If you live with a person with BPD who attacks you verbally, threatens to injure you, or threatens self-injury or suicide, *you* may experience severe and traumatic invalidation. Many have suffered trauma and post-traumatic stress from the behaviors of a family member with BPD. You may need to seek safety and support for your trauma.

BPD can be generational. Some parents and spouses of a person with BPD grew up with a mother or father with a personality disorder. Perhaps you suffered chronic invalidation, emotional neglect, or trauma in your own childhood. While you may or may not meet the criteria for BPD, you may be short of the resilience and persistence needed to manage another difficult relationship effectively. Post-traumatic stress disorder (PTSD) is actually a normal response to traumatic events (van der Kolk 2014).

"Problem Behavior"

DBT understands emotional dysregulation to be at the core of borderline personality disorder. However, experiencing an intense emotion might not be a problem at all. The priority for DBT treatment is usually the impulsive, problematic behavior that occurs as a result of emotional dysregulation.

Impulsive behavior is taking an action without planning and without considering the medium- or long-term consequences. The most dangerous impulsive behaviors appear when a person is in an intense emotional state and urgently wants immediate relief. Impulsive behavior is a way to eliminate the feeling quickly. It can happen without thinking or awareness. Only the immediate consequences matter. Examples of problematic, impulsive behavior include:

- attacking verbally, including yelling, insults, blame, profanity, condescending sarcasm, etc.

- binge eating

- consuming drugs or alcohol

- threatening suicide

- breaking things

- excessive spending on unnecessary and unaffordable things

- self-cutting or other self-injury

- aggressive driving

- physically attacking others

- attempting suicide

While impulsive behaviors are the most notable forms of behavioral instability in BPD, compulsive behaviors, avoidant behaviors, and active passivity may also become part of a person's repertoire as a response to chronic negative feelings.

Compulsive behavior is associated with an urge to do it repeatedly—until a feeling of anxiety or unease goes away. Eating, exercising, shopping, gambling, consuming drugs, checking and posting on social media, or even talking excessively with little tolerance for other points of view, can all be examples of compulsive behaviors.

Avoidant behaviors may include sleeping all day, not leaving a bedroom, and "icing" or "stonewalling" loved ones with the silent treatment. In addition, refusing to attend school, chronic absenteeism from work, long-term unemployment without looking for work, and disengagement from friends or social activities are other types of avoidant behaviors.

Active passivity is the tendency to respond helplessly to life's problems. It can overlap with avoidant behaviors. Active passivity specifically involves complaining about something without solving a problem, acting helpless, or wishing that others fix a problem—without asking. It may also appear as an insistent demand for others to solve their problems.

• *Simon and Elena*

Simon was twenty and lived with his mom, Elena, who was unpredictable and emotionally reactive. He was counting the months until he graduated and got a job. When Simon came home from class one day, he told his mom that a friend's family was giving away a perfectly good refrigerator. His mother had been complaining about their very old one for years and, as a single mom, she could not afford a new one.

Elena started anxiously telling him everything she needed fixed around the house and criticizing Simon for never helping. As she grew increasingly furious, the volume of her voice escalated. Simon tried to calm her. Finally, she swept her arm across the dining table where he and his brother usually studied, sending glasses, books, and food flying. He was accustomed to his mother's outbursts, but he was still shocked and scared that his mom reacted that way after he was delivering good news and being helpful.

What exactly were Elena's impulsive and problematic behaviors? Feeling anxious or angry are not behaviors. Being worried about repairs needed around the house is not a behavioral problem. Criticizing, yelling, and breaking things were the impulsive problem behaviors.

exercise: Problem Behaviors

Consider how good news turned so bad. What activated Elena's fury? What do you think was the "last straw" that triggered her impulsive behavior, which resulted in food flying?

_____

_____

_____

_____

_____

Now, consider your loved one's impulsive or problematic behaviors—behaviors that threaten life or health, interfere with life goals, and are obstacles to developing and sustaining the quality of life your loved one desires.

As you write, be sure to separate behaviors from thoughts and feelings. Describe observable actions! Only include behaviors you observed in your loved one within the past three to four months. Keep in mind, getting angry is _not_ a problem behavior, but insulting someone is a problem behavior. Being unable to sleep is _not_ a problem behavior, but chatting on social media all night _is_ a problem behavior. Skipping meals _may or may not_ be a problem behavior. Not separating the white clothes from the dark clothes when doing the laundry is _not_ a problem behavior of the type that we are concerned with here. (Although we can all get overwhelmed, burned out, and lose sight of discerning the difference between problem behaviors and pet peeves!)

List the problem behaviors of your loved one:

_____

_____

_____

_____

_____

Now, list your own problem behaviors. Some common examples may include yelling, reckless driving, drinking alcohol, interrupting others, or shutting them out with the silent treatment for hours or even days.

_____

_____

_____

_____

_____

Look back at your lists of problem behaviors. Check to make sure they are observable behaviors.

Rewrite both lists in priority order, from the most important problem behavior to change, to the least important behavior to change.

_____

_____

_____

_____

_____

_____

Summary

The biosocial theory of emotional dysregulation says that it is caused by the interaction of emotional vulnerability (biological) and chronic invalidation (social). Emotional dysregulation manifests in various realms, including interpersonal (loving and hating others), cognitive (expectation of rejection), behavioral (impulsivity), and identity (unstable inner experience and emptiness). Understanding the complexity of this condition can help families begin to stop minimizing and invalidating a loved one with chronic and severe emotional dysregulation.

CHAPTER 2

The Wisdom of Presence and Acceptance

Presence and acceptance are fundamental to social connection, healthy relationships, and emotional stability. *Presence* is being fully aware of what is happening as it happens. It is the ability to pay close attention to other people, our surroundings, and our inner experience without going down all those mental rabbit holes of distraction. *Acceptance* allows reality to be just as it is, without judgment, criticism, or automatic attempts to change it. Acceptance can relieve endless problem-solving effort, resentment, and exhaustion. Being present and accepting will give you greater clarity and wisdom to navigate your life and interactions with others.

The most fundamental element of DBT, *mindfulness*, cultivates presence and acceptance. Mindfulness improves concentration, perceptual clarity, and emotional stability as it relieves mental distress (Young 2016).

Before diving into mindfulness skills, let's meet Rina, who is struggling with her daughter, Jessi. Later in the chapter, we will explore how mindfulness skills can help an anxious mom and her self-harming daughter.

• *Rina and Jessi*

Jessi is in her second year of college and has struggled with self-harm for years. After a few months of DBT, Jessi reduced the frequency of her self-cutting, but nobody convinced her to give it up. Jessi used to show off the cuts, receiving lots of attention from her mom. Since

Rina began to respond without any warmth to the injuries (following instructions from her daughter's therapist), Jessi stopped telling Rina when she cut herself. Rina has suffered anxiety for years, which results in Jessi avoiding her mother even more. Jessi's absence only makes Rina more anxious! Can Rina break this cycle? How can something as esoteric as "presence and acceptance" help Jessi stop cutting herself and help Rina reduce anxiety?

self-reflection: Automatic Reactions

Consider a situation in which you reacted automatically, such as raising your voice, correcting, giving advice, slamming a door, or driving aggressively. What did you do?

_____

_____

_____

_____

_____

Recall any automatic judgments or mental criticism that accompanied your reaction and write them down.

_____

_____

_____

_____

_____

You may not have been the only person emotionally aroused. However, did your automatic reaction make the situation better or worse? How?

_____

_____

_____

_____

_____

Is there anything you might do differently, if you could go back in time or if it were to happen again?

_____

_____

_____

_____

_____

_____

Core Mindfulness Skills

Mindfulness gets us out of the automatic reactions and judgmental criticisms. Mindfulness is paying attention to what is happening in the present moment, here and now. It's being aware of what we are doing when we are doing it. On one hand, this is effortless. Just listen. Can you hear that sound? How much effort was involved in directing your attention to hearing? Almost zero? On the other hand, it does require some discipline and practice.

There are six core skills: three attitudes (How Skills) that support acceptance and presence, and three practices (What Skills) to direct and sustain attention (Linehan 1993).

How Skill 1: Let Go of Judgment

Did you ever notice how your mind can make endless automatic judgments that lead to personal distress and interpersonal conflict? The speed at which our minds jump to conclusions or make assumptions is so fast that we don't even realize what is happening as it happens. Only later it might become apparent. Letting go of judgments can begin with changing speaking and thinking habits. For example:

Judgment: *There is nothing but crap on TV.*

Replace with description: *I don't enjoy watching television. I prefer watching a streaming service.*

Judgment: *He is a stubborn (*#%@!). It's a waste of time to argue with him.*

Replace with description: *If I disagree with him, it is unlikely to change his mind.*

How Skill 2: Attend to One Thing at a Time

Multitasking and distractions both reduce mental productivity and increase mistakes. Let go of distractions or the urge to multitask, and bring your attention back to the task at hand, again and again.

Practice attending to one thing at a time with a cup of coffee, tea, or cold drink. While sipping it, notice things like the weight of the cup, the color, smell, flavor, temperature of the liquid, and even the sound of swallowing.

Practice listening to another person with your eyes, ears, and heart. Let go of any distractions. Stop trying to figure out what you will say when they finish speaking and, instead, listen. Pay full attention to what the other person is communicating and experiencing.

How Skill 3: Be Effective

Being effective means doing what works. Remember what's important. Keep the big picture in mind. Act skillfully and remember your objectives, aspirations, and values.

For example, when you say or do something that activates a loved one's emotional reaction, and you want to de-escalate the situation, it's usually more effective to just listen and validate instead of explaining or defending yourself.

If you are hurt or angry about something someone said, ask yourself, *How can I be effective here?* Depending on what you want and need, being effective might mean letting it go, asking what they meant, or saying that it hurt your feelings.

The task is to remember and practice the following in your daily life: a nonjudgmental attitude, doing one thing at a time, and being effective.

exercise: Practice Your How Skills

Write three judgmental things you frequently say and then rewrite them without judgment or criticism, being honest and specific about the facts. Upon rereading them, is there any difference in how you feel after reading the more judgmental comment compared to the judgment-free text?

_____

_____

_____

_____

Take five or ten minutes to do just one thing, such as eating or drinking, walking, listening to music or a podcast, talking on the phone, or any activity you might otherwise get distracted from or multitask around. Write down what you did, how it felt, and what you might do differently, if anything, as a result.

_____

_____

_____

_____

_____

When you are slightly activated emotionally (at a low intensity), ask yourself, *What would the most effective thing to do right now be?* Try doing it. Write about the experience and how it worked out.

_____

_____

_____

_____

_____

What Skill 1: Observe

We observe via our five senses (see, hear, feel, taste, and smell) that connect us to the world. We also have the ability to perceive our thoughts. These can be visual images that we "see" in our mind or an internal dialogue that we "hear" in our mind.

To practice observing, focus on pure sensation—without any added concepts, without naming the sound you hear or see. Just to perceive what you see, hear, feel, and so on, is the most basic of all the mindfulness practices. The following exercise will guide you on a tour of observing, one by one, each of the seven senses.

self-reflection: Observe

Read each paragraph below, then pause and try observing as instructed.

Close your eyes and listen to whatever sounds arise. There's no need to label where the sound comes from. Just listen. Notice the volume, pitch, and rhythm. Listen closely. Notice if there's silence between the sounds. Notice how you can never predict with certainty what the next sound will be.

Then, open your eyes. Just observe with your eyes and let go of any inner dialogue that arises about what you see. There's no need to identify objects. Just notice colors, textures, shapes, light, or shadow. Take your time. Look around as if it's the first time you could see. Look for things you never noticed before, even if it's a scratch or a crack.

Next, notice what's touching your skin. Feel the texture of fabric against your skin. There may be a place where your clothing is tight and another where it is loose. Notice where you feel warmth or coolness (perhaps in hands or feet), dryness (lips), or wetness (interior of the mouth). Notice if you can feel the air passing over the skin where nothing touches it (nostrils or base of the upper lip).

With each inhale, notice if there is a smell or a fragrance in the room or on your clothes or skin. Then, see if your mouth has any taste or flavor, perhaps left over from the last thing you ate or drank.

Now check inside. Is there any muscular tension in your body? Observe that for a moment, breathing in and out. Notice the expansion and relaxation of the lower ribs. Notice if relaxing more deeply on the next few out-breaths is possible. Move your shoulders. Stretch. Just notice the physical sensations as you gently move.

Finally, shift to your seventh sense, your ability to perceive your thoughts. Close your eyes and put your attention behind your forehead. Sit still for a few minutes. Notice if thoughts arise. If you would like, generate ideas and observe them. They may be mental images (imagining the face of a loved one) or mental audio (thinking, *This is a thought*). Remain aware of mental experience without getting lost in thought (Siegal 2022).

So how was the tour of your seven senses? Did you notice anything new? Some people find some senses easier to observe, or more enjoyable, pleasant, or relaxing than others. Was there anything that you especially appreciated? Did you find the overall experience calming or activating?

_____

_____

_____

_____

_____

_____

◆ *Simon and Elena*

Simon usually got home at night feeling stressed and tired. After a long day, he had no energy left for his unpredictable mother, Elena. Simon decided to focus more on himself instead of worrying about her. He practiced the Observe Skill on his way home. He stretched before getting into his car. He paused and observed his breath before starting the car. He kept the radio off, drove slower, and tried to be a more considerate and mindful driver on his way home. He arrived home, sat in his car, closed his eyes, and observed how he felt. When he entered the house, he had far less anxiety and could calmly greet his mother.

What Skill 2: Describe

Describe what you see, hear, or feel. Describe without judgment, exaggeration, or confusing evaluations with facts. Accurately describing your experience can be a powerful support to help you stay grounded in the present.

◆ *Carrie and Larry*

Carrie was telling a friend about her son. When he wanted something, "Larry the Lamborghini" went from zero to sixty in a few seconds. "He wants to make me feel bad! He is looking for ways to hurt me! He screams at me and insults me…and it's never going to get better!"

Carrie was anxious, and her friend was confused. Then Carrie remembered the Describe Skill. She began again, more slowly saying, "Larry asked me if he could have some cookies, and I told him that he could have a banana." Choosing her words carefully and speaking calmly, she continued, "He screamed that he hates bananas and started banging the kitchen cupboards, yelling and swearing at me. Then he ran upstairs. A few minutes later, he came back to show me that he was putting chocolate into his mouth." Carrie imitated his exaggerated gesture. "He found the last piece of dark chocolate that I hid in my bedroom." A weak smile came to her face. "It really wasn't much sugar," she added.

Carrie moved out of her emotional state as she let go of judgments and accurately described what happened in a relaxed and neutral voice. She was even open to seeing the humor by staging Larry's dramatic gesture as he ate the last bite of chocolate!

exercise: Practice Observe and Describe Skills

Observing and describing keep us firmly rooted in the present moment. Try one of these or create another practice to observe and describe your experience.

- Observe and describe feelings, for example, "I am feeling impatient and have an urge to move more quickly."

- Describe what you see. Find something in nature, for example, a leaf or a drop of water, and describe it in as much concrete detail as possible, without any judgments or evaluations.

Write down what you did and how it helped you become grounded in the present moment.

_____

_____

_____

_____

_____

_____

What Skill 3: Participate

Participating means entering into the experience. Become one with the experience. Just do it. Participating can come naturally while playing sports, singing, playing an instrument, dancing, making art, or even at work when you are deeply engaged in it.

◆ *Serena and Cedric*

It was a rainy morning, and Cedric was feeling down. Serena could not tolerate his pessimism. She had lots of things she wanted to do. She could sense resentment arising. She decided to try a Participate Skill and share it with her husband. She found her favorite song, "Happy" by Pharrell Williams, on her cell phone and played it. She began to smile and move with the music, then started dancing and singing. She waved at Cedric to dance with her. To her surprise, he stood and moved to the music. When the song finished, she applauded and hugged him. Those three minutes regulated her emotions. She could say, cheerfully and firmly, that she had a lot of things to do and wouldn't be able to chat over coffee that morning.

exercise: Practice Participating

Choose one of the following activities to try.

- Put earphones on and play a favorite song loudly. Sing along without any care about being in tune or not!

- Play happy music and dance when nobody is watching, just fully attending to the music and the movements.

- Close your eyes and deeply savor one piece of a favorite food: one potato chip, a piece of chocolate, one spoonful of ice cream, or one bit of any delicious food. Let it melt in your mouth or chew until it is liquid, listening to each crunch, feeling texture and temperature, savoring every aspect.

What experience did you participate fully in, and what did you notice in this experience?

_____

_____

_____

_____

_____

_____

Weave the six Core Mindfulness Skills into daily life! Pay attention to what you are doing when you are doing it through observing, describing, or participating. Remember the importance of being nonjudgmental, attending to one thing at a time, and being effective (instead of needing to be right!).

• *Rina and Jessi*

Rina began to take a few minutes every morning to be more present. While drinking her morning coffee, she stopped listening to the news and cleaning the kitchen. Instead, Rina began to pay full attention to her coffee. Between sips, she just observed her thoughts, her coffee, and her cat.

At first, she was present with the discomfort of not doing other things, of feeling agitated, of thinking it was a waste of time. She also observed that sometimes, later in the morning, she felt free of anxiety after taking that quiet time!

Jessi was in college and lived at home. She had started online DBT classes and knew about the Core Mindfulness Skills. One day, she was anxious, irritated, and on the verge of cutting herself. Jessi observed that she was also hungry and decided to eat first and see how she felt afterward. Rina gave her daughter money to get fast food delivered. Jessi continued to practice observing the progress of her order on the app while she waited for it to arrive.

When the food came, she ate it mindfully. The urge to cut herself had passed by the time she finished eating.

self-reflection: Mindful Eating

Rina and Jessi found mindful eating to have beneficial consequences. Take a moment to consider committing to eating or drinking something mindfully every day. What would you do? How would you do it?

_____

_____

_____

_____

_____

_____

_____

Practicing Acceptance

Acceptance recognizes "that which is" with a disposition of openness and flexibility. It can be quite challenging to accept reality as it is, especially when it doesn't meet our expectations or desires. For those who are emotionally vulnerable, rejecting reality can escalate into a howling outrage of denial or a bottomless pit of despair.

Accepting reality does not mean liking it. It is allowing truth to be just as it is. It is giving up the fight and the longing for it to be different. It can be emotionally painful to let go of the hope that others will behave as you would like or to feel what you want them to feel.

Some people confuse acceptance with resignation. Letting go of insisting that *things should be different* and loosening your grip on attempts to control things is not resignation. Resignation implies giving up and passively allowing whatever will happen to happen. But acceptance is being present with reality just as it is. Knowing that the present situation will change and evolve, you will be present to respond appropriately as the situation changes.

◆ *Marsha*

Marsha Linehan acknowledged that the best gift from her mother was her faith. A year after being discharged from residential treatment, she was at a Catholic retreat center. Marsha walked into the chapel feeling deeply sad and hopeless. She kneeled at the altar to pray. Suddenly she felt intense joy. She looked up, and everything around her seemed to shimmer with gold. After a few minutes, she ran back to her room. She went to the mirror and said aloud, "I love myself."

Years later, Marsha recalled what had changed for her in that moment: "I accepted myself as I was." Until then, the difference between who she was and who she wanted to be had been so vast that her life was unbearable. She called it "radical acceptance." It saved her life. She never considered another suicide attempt, and she never cut herself again (Carey 2011).

◆ *Rina, Joshua, and Jessi*

Rina and Joshua both tried to completely accept their daughter, Jessi, just as she was—frequently unhappy, dysregulated, and self-cutting. "The truth is that I tried to control my daughter to relieve my anxiety and fulfill my expectations. I could never control her, and the struggle got worse than ever," Rina said. "It took time, but once I accepted her self-cutting, I stopped freaking out. Now I just ask her if she has bandages or needs to get stitches."

Joshua had daily conversations with Jessi that lasted over an hour while she criticized her mother or needed money to solve a problem. One day, he realized that he was not accepting reality. "I just want her to be happy. I'm always bailing her out and she never learns from her mistakes. Clearly, it hasn't made her any happier; it's just sustaining the problem." He calmly communicated a boundary with Jessi around the amount of money he was comfortable giving her, and set a personal boundary with himself around the length of time he was willing to listen to Jessi's complaints each day.

Acceptance of a situation might result in you changing your behavior, just like Joshua.

Wise Mind

In DBT, the goal of practicing mindfulness is to connect with your Wise Mind by integrating Emotional Mind and Rational Mind.

Emotional Mind hijacks thoughts, words, voice, and actions according to the emotion. It can be a rollercoaster of highs and lows with lots of drama. *Rational Mind* denies, suppresses, or ignores emotions. Only logic and facts matter. In Rational Mind, there may be little pleasure or empathy and lots of pragmatic reasoning. Emotional Mind is hot. Rational Mind is cold.

Wise Mind integrates and balances Emotional Mind and Rational Mind. *Wise Mind* considers the knowledge and insights that come from physical sensations, sensory perception, emotional feelings, facts, logical reasoning, and values. Wise Mind is intuitive and thoughtfully reflective. Mindfulness moves us toward Wise Mind. To connect with your Wise Mind, take a few mindful breaths and then ask yourself, *Am I in Wise Mind?* If you find you are in Emotional Mind or Rational Mind, try practicing a couple of the Core Mindfulness Skills for five or ten minutes and then check in again.

◆ *Serena and Cedric*

Cedric had retired from investment banking. At home all day, he began exploding around his wife in a rage that included yelling and profanity, then leaving the house for hours. He would return as if nothing had happened and did not want to discuss it. Yet he never wanted Serena to leave the house without him.

Serena decided she would radically accept that Cedric could not control his anger. He is how he is, she thought. She stopped trying to talk it out in the hope of convincing him to change his ways.

Serena took time to connect with her Wise Mind. She sat quietly for a while and attended to her breath. Now that she accepted that Cedric's behavioral patterns were not something she could change, she asked her Wise Mind what to do.

She saw herself all alone, walking on the beach, listening to the surf and the seagulls. She felt a deep sense of peace and safety.

With that, she made a calm and grounded decision to separate. A few days later, she explained this to Cedric from a place of wisdom, not criticism. For the first time in his adult life, Cedric offered to do therapy—both couples counseling and individual therapy. Serena was shocked and took some time alone to check in again with her Wise Mind. She needed a break and did not totally trust Cedric. Once again, Wise Mind advised her. Serena told him that she still wanted a temporary separation, and that she would move back in after, not before, he completed three months of therapy.

self-reflection: Wise Mind

If you are facing a decision and feeling anxious or confused, try asking your Wise Mind. Find a quiet space where you can sit comfortably for a few minutes without interruption.

Observe the breath in its natural state without trying to control it. Notice the moment when the inhale stops, and the exhale begins. Notice the pause at the end of the exhale before the next inhale. Carefully attend to that experience repeatedly at each breath's top and bottom.

After five minutes, inhale deeply and ask your Wise Mind a question. On the exhale, listen for an answer. Don't give yourself an answer; just listen to your inner experience.

Some good questions for Wise Mind might include: "What should I do?" "How should I respond?" "How can I be more effective?" Or, "What do I want out of this interaction?"

Did an answer arise? Did you have a sense of Wise Mind? What gave you that sense?

_____

_____

_____

_____

Was the response a wise one? Why or why not?

_____

_____

_____

_____

Would you do anything different the next time you ask Wise Mind a question?

_____

_____

_____

_____

Sometimes, there will be a sense of centeredness or clear insight. That's your Wise Mind. Sometimes, no answers arise. Try again later. If it needs to be clarified whether an answer came from Wise Mind, see if the response has a comprehensive perspective or considers long-term consequences. You can always reflect upon the solution or try again later.

Summary

The six Core Mindfulness Skills, along with Acceptance and Wise Mind, can and should be practiced daily. It takes no extra time to pay attention to what you are doing when you are doing it, to be less judgmental, or to apply any other mindfulness skill in daily life. These skills will reduce your stress, improve interpersonal relationships, and connect you with your Wise Mind. You will experience a greater sense of wellness as you mindfully cultivate more presence and acceptance.

CHAPTER 3

Understanding Emotions

When you have a loved one who is emotionally vulnerable or reactive, you need an extra dose of emotional intelligence! You need to be competent at understanding and managing your own emotions to recognize, empathize, and hold space for another's emotions. If mindfulness is the most fundamental DBT skill, *mindfulness of emotions* is a close second.

A person's emotional dysregulation is often activated by those who are closest. Making matters even more painful, emotional reactions in intimate relationships are often reciprocal and quickly escalate into hostility and hurt feelings on both sides. As you probably know, this happens even if you are just trying to calm the situation!

Emotions arise when the central nervous system and bloodstream are flooded with electrical energy, neurochemicals, and hormones. They can surge so quickly that we are unaware of them and don't realize what is happening until they begin to subside. People with exceptional emotional competence might experience a delay of only a few seconds before they realize it. Others can have difficulty making sense of their emotions even after days of ruminating or obsessive thinking.

Changing how you respond to your loved one will change how they respond to you. You need to be your own best guide and navigate your emotions without blaming your loved one for your feelings, just as you want them to do for you.

◆ *Simon, Ivan, and Elena*

Simon and Ivan were twins who both attended a local college. Yet they had very different relationships with their emotionally sensitive mother, Elena. Simon tried so hard to please.

He maintained her car, helped with the bills from his part-time job, and did minor repairs around the house. When their mom was irritated, Simon was anxious about his mother's unpredictable emotional reactions. Out of anxiety, he was more likely to reason with her to calm her down, give her advice, or even try to solve her problem. Sometimes, he would react with impatience, nervousness, or even fear. He had good reason to be afraid. He had been yelled at and unfairly criticized. She had even thrown something at him more than once.

Ivan was around their mother far less. He was more likely to be calm and relaxed in her presence. Ivan listened without interruption when she started ranting and complaining. He did not take what she said personally, accepted her with all her emotional ups and downs, and often validated her feelings with genuine warmth and kindness. When validation did not seem to help sustain a positive conversation, Ivan changed the subject or left the house. On some occasions, her response might be a snarky comment. He always ignored it and left her with a quick hug. Ivan had more emotional regulation skills than his brother. It was not perfect, but Ivan's interactions with his mother rarely escalated.

self-reflection: Interpersonal Relationship Variations

Consider your relationship with your loved one. Now, think about others in your family and how your relationship with them differs. Then consider: Is there another family member who has less conflict with your difficult loved one because they respond with more emotional balance and flexibility—or perhaps they are just a little more distant? Is there something for you to learn from their interactions? Or is it possible that your loved one has become more isolated and you are accommodating their isolation by filling too many of their needs? Reflect on this in writing.

_____

_____

_____

_____

_____

_____

Why Do We Have Emotions?

Emotions are products of human evolution. They motivate us to move toward or away, be tense or relaxed, focus attention or widen perspective. Emotions inform us that something is happening that is relevant to our health, safety, or well-being—and our logical brains may not even be aware of it. It is possible to sense that something is not right long before we have cognitive knowledge of what is wrong. The sensations and urges of each emotion have a specific function (Ekman 2007; Linehan 2015). For example:

- **Anger**—Attack to defend against threats or eliminate obstacles that stand in the way of desires or objectives.

- **Awe and surprise**—Stop, assess, connect, and learn.

- **Contempt**—Push down and away people or actions morally inferior to yourself or your group. Strengthen ties within the tribe and cut ties with outsiders.

- **Disgust**—Push away anything that may be physically toxic, offensive, or immoral.

- **Envy**—Try harder, compete, and progress.

- **Fear**—Avoid and escape predators, threats, or danger.

- **Guilt**—Repair the damage of an action that violated your own values.

- **Jealousy**—Ensure the reproduction of your own genes (men) or ensure help and protection with child care (women).

- **Joy**—Improve health and longevity.

- **Love**—Reproduction, child care, mutual cooperation, and group cohesion.

- **Sadness**—Recover and reorganize yourself or your life after a loss. Receive help.

- **Shame**—Avoid being rejected by your family or tribe by hiding transgressions or appeasing others.

Emotions communicate information to the self and motivate urges and actions, but emotional information is not always reliable. You must check the facts. For example, a young man asserted that he knew his girlfriend was cheating on him because he was jealous. With further introspection, he realized that he had no real evidence. He was afraid of being alone and felt jealous in most of his relationships.

Our emotions also communicate information to others. The tone of voice, gestures, and facial expressions communicate to and influence others. If you see a person looking down, shoulders hunched, and about to cry, you will feel and respond very differently than if you see the same person looking at you intensely with eyes narrowed, eyebrows furrowed, and lips pursed. Emotions are transactional—the presence of another person who is emotionally activated is sure to affect you, and vice versa.

◆ *Carrie and Larry*

Carrie was afraid of her son, Larry, at thirteen. Without warning and in less than one minute, he could go from calm, smiling, and chatty to enraged and screaming. When he was six, Carrie called him "Larry the Lamborghini," but as a teenager it was not funny. Larry was as tall as Carrie and weighed more. The screaming meltdowns were terrifying.

Larry could be reactive and stubborn toward almost anyone, but when Carrie was present, his defiance and aggression were off the charts. Carrie's fear caused her to be hypervigilant when her son was around. She resented him, which made her feel guilty. Larry the Lamborghini was ruining her life.

One day, after feeling frozen with fear when her son began a meltdown over what she was serving for dinner, she began to reflect upon the situation. She was on high alert whenever she was alone with him. Was it possible that her fear was somehow influencing Larry? If she could regulate her fear, would he coregulate with her? She did not know, but she decided to process her fear better—for both of them.

Primary and Secondary Emotions

A primary emotion is a physiological response that lasts until all the electricity, neurochemicals, and hormones clear from the nervous system and the bloodstream. That takes about ninety seconds! So why does it seem that our emotions can last for hours? Thinking can keep our emotions alive for much longer (Taylor 2008). Thoughts and feelings interact to sustain emotions. We can ruminate obsessively or replay a dialogue in our heads, thus maintaining a negative emotion all day. It can be a vicious circle. On the other hand, many feelings are subtle, and we unconsciously regulate them by mentally letting go and redirecting attention.

Secondary emotions are reactions to primary emotions, which are appropriate to the context. Believing an emotion to be "bad" or "intolerable" automatically provokes a secondary emotion. For example, ignoring the primary emotion and reacting with anger can be an unconscious habit. Anger and sadness are both common secondary emotions triggered by other painful feelings that are suppressed or avoided by moving into the secondary emotion.

Some clinicians and researchers in psychology believe that anger toward a loved one is always secondary. How could that be? The theory goes that if you have no judgments, interpretations, or criticism when a primary emotion is activated, the actions of a loved one would not trigger anger because this is a person you love and care about (Fruzzetti 2006).

◆ *Phoebe and Daphne*

Phoebe was resentful that her daughter, Daphne, had cut her off from her grandchildren. She had no idea what her infraction was and Daphne would not tell her. It had been two months, and it felt totally unfair. She was angry.

On the other hand, when she relaxed and thought about her grandkids, anger would melt completely and tears would come to her eyes. She realized sadness was the primary emotion and anger was a secondary emotion.

self-reflection: Primary and Secondary Emotions

Give some thought to the last time you were angry or sad. Consider whether there might have been an underlying emotion. Were you disappointed over what happened? Were you feeling disrespected or shamed? Was there envy or disgust? Maybe you were mad at yourself (a secondary emotion) instead of feeling guilty (a possible primary emotion). Reflect on your primary emotion in writing.

_____

_____

_____

_____

_____

_____

Naming the Emotion

Words matter. Become familiar with terms that indicate variations in intensity within each "family" of emotions. Build a bigger vocabulary for your feelings and name your emotions often.

Accurate expression lessens the pain, helps you accept your emotions, and allows the arising and passing of emotional experience. Acting out your feelings or suppressing, ignoring, or blaming others increases emotional suffering. When you accurately express your feelings, you model effective emotional expression to your loved one. In addition, you will be helping yourself experience more equanimity and less emotional suffering.

The following figure illustrates facial expressions of emotions (Eckman 2007) and lists three words that are variations of each emotion. Try to describe your feelings more often, using words such as these. (You'll find a treasury of information about your emotions in the free tools offered online.)

Twelve Basic Families of Emotions

Sadness

Discouraged			
Disappointed			
Hurt			

Fear

Worried
Anxious
Panicked

Anger

Frustrated
Annoyed
Resentful

Awe/Surprise

Wonder
Astonished
Amazed

Contempt

Disrespectful
Snarky
Indignant

Shame

Vulnerable
Inadequate
Humiliated

Joy

Satisfied
Happy
Excited

Love

Interested
Attracted
Adoring

Guilt

Apologetic
Regretful
Remorseful

Jealousy

Possessive
Clingy
Controlling

Envy

Craving
Rivalry
Covetous

Disgust

Dislike
Aversion
Repugnant

Mindfulness of Emotions

Many automatic reactions arise from the urge to escape an emotional experience immediately. When emotions seem overwhelming and uncontrollable, it can feel like only two options exist: either engage in urgent and intense emotional expression, including maladaptive behavior and messy interpersonal conflict, or avoid and isolate to repress feelings, inhibit urges, and prevent problem behaviors. Although it may seem counterintuitive, the practice of accepting and acknowledging feelings reduces insecurity and increases self-competence and self-knowledge.

exercise: Mindfully Observe an Emotion

Pick a moment when something occurs that is only a little disappointing, frustrating, or embarrassing—not too intense. Building emotional competence requires introspective inquiry and mindful attention during and after emotional experiences. Negative thinking usually indicates that an aversive emotion is present. When you notice some negative thoughts, that might be another good time to pause and do this practice.

Observe Your Emotion: Observe the emotion without judging, rejecting, or clinging to it. Welcome the emotion by saying "Hello" to your emotion and then name it, even if it's an unexpected and unpleasant guest. Accept and respect what you feel; it is your body's present physiological state. Practice loving your emotions!

Fully Connect Mind and Body: Pay attention to your breath. Breathe slightly deeper and more slowly. Exhale tension from the body with each breath. After a minute, imagine the body surrendering to gravity with each exhale.

Note precisely what physical sensations are present. Feel what you feel with patience and curiosity. Pay attention to sensations in your face, neck, shoulders, chest, abdomen, and extremities. Take your time and look for sensations that are even more subtle by asking, *What else is there?* Notice urges to act or speak without acting upon the urges.

Observe the Wave: Remember: You are not your emotion. This, too, will pass. Notice how long it takes for the emotion to go down or remember moments you have felt differently.

Write down how this practice went and describe how it might have helped you connect, accept, or regulate the emotion.

_____

_____

_____

_____

_____

_____

_____

Did you find it useful? Rate its usefulness on a scale of 1 (not useful at all) to 5 (very useful).

_____

_____

If this mindfulness exercise was hard or if you have trouble identifying your emotions, carefully look through the following table. Identifying your emotion can be a process of observing your inner experience, including the thoughts that arise in your mind and the physical sensations in your body.

Sample Thoughts and Sensations for Twelve Emotions

	Thoughts	Sensations
Anger	*That's so unfair. It's all your fault.*	tension, urge to attack
Awe/Surprise	*Wow! That's amazing!*	stillness, openness, expansion
Contempt	*When I do it, it's done right. He'll just mess it up.*	feeling taller, lighter, nausea
Disgust	*He is such a liar and takes credit for other people's work. I stay away.*	feelings of nausea or suffocation, contamination, urge to wash
Envy	*I want that. I deserve it. She gets everything.*	tension in the neck and jaw, pain in the gut, rigidity in the body
Fear	*I'm so worried about money. What if I lose my job?*	tension, agitation, heart pounding, urge to avoid
Guilt	*I am so sorry. It was my mistake. Please forgive me.*	heat, discomfort, impulse to punish self or please others
Jealousy	*You're always paying attention to her.*	lack of air, accelerated heart rate, choking, clinginess
Joy	*Everything is good. I am safe and loved.*	expansion of chest or body, lightness, connection
Love	*She is so nice and she likes me.*	feeling expansion in the chest, energized, confident
Sadness	*I can't do anything right. I'm such a failure.*	heaviness, urge to isolate and rest
Shame	*Everybody thinks I'm a failure.*	body heat, stomach pain, urge to disappear

Describe and Deconstruct an Emotion

Another fundamental skill for increasing emotional competence is the practice of describing and deconstructing emotions. The following outline explains this practice.

Name the Emotion and Its Intensity: Naming an emotion and noting the intensity when it was at its peak from 1 (least intense) to 10 (most intense) may help to regulate the emotion.

Vulnerability Factors: These are factors that reduce the threshold for activating an emotion. Poor sleep often makes us more sensitive to sadness. Hunger increases our vulnerability to getting angry (also known as being "hangry"). Hormonal changes during menstruation can increase emotional vulnerability and reactivity.

Activating Event: The activating event provokes the emotion. Were it not for the activating event, the emotional reaction would not have happened at that moment. It may be something that another says or does, or it may be an internal thought or sensation that activates the emotion.

Thoughts or Interpretations of the Event: Mental activity around the activating event charges or changes the emotional reaction. If someone steps on your foot and you think it was intentional, you might react angrily. If the same action occurred, but you believe the person is lame or blind, you might react with guilt.

Sensations: Physical sensations are the most essential aspect of an emotion. Sensations may include: feelings in the chest or stomach; muscular tension in the jaw, shoulders, or other places in the body; feelings of tingling, lightness, heaviness, pain, or energy.

Urges to Act or Speak: The most fundamental urges are to move forward, away, up or down, or an impulse to speak or act without necessarily saying or doing anything.

Behaviors: Words, gestures, and actions are all behaviors that can be hijacked by an emotion. Changes in facial expression, posture, tone of voice, volume, or speed of speech all communicate an emotion.

Consequences or Residual Aftereffects: A secondary emotion may arise as a reaction to a primary emotion. Lingering sensations such as pain, tension, or discomfort may last hours. Memory may be affected, including lapses, flashbacks, or the inability to stop thinking about what happened.

• *Fatima and Aisha*

Fatima described an incident with her adult daughter. "Aisha called to ask if I could dog-sit for the weekend. I said yes, but explained that I would ask her father to pick up the dog for me because I had to help my other daughter. Aisha started insulting me, saying I only cared about her sister, and then hung up. I didn't know what to say or do. I was in shock. After a while, I decided to describe and deconstruct what I felt."

Name of emotion: *Fear*

Intensity (rated on a scale of 1 to 10): 6

Vulnerability Factors: *Tired from an intense week at work.*

Activating Event: *Aisha's outburst, which led her to suddenly hang up on me.*

Thoughts/Interpretations: *I didn't know what to think. My mind was momentarily blank.*

Sensations: *It felt like I had been punched in the stomach. I felt shocked, paralyzed.*

Action Urges: *Part of me wanted just to hang up the phone.*

Behaviors (words and actions): *I did not say or do anything immediately.*

Aftereffects: *Secondary emotion, sadness. I felt my throat tighten and tears well up in my eyes.*

exercise: Deconstruct and Describe an Emotion

Select a recent experience that activated a mild emotion. Don't start with a long or intense emotion, or you may not get through the exercise. You can download free tools online that offer support material to help you with this important exercise.

Emotion: _____

Intensity (rated on a scale of 1 to 10): _____

Vulnerability Factors: _____

_____

Activating Event (be specific): _____

_____

_____

Thoughts/Interpretations: _____

_____

_____

Sensations: _____

_____

_____

Actions Urges: _____

_____

_____

Behaviors (words and actions): _____

_____

_____

Aftereffects: _____

_____

_____

_____

Summary

Understanding emotions is necessary to regulate yourself and to coregulate, validate, and communicate effectively. Emotions motivate thoughts and actions, and inform you about matters relevant to your health, safety, and well-being. Connecting to your inner experience and being able to express that experience in nonjudgmental language builds greater emotional competence.

Mindfulness of emotions is a set of skills for experiencing and processing an emotion without over- or underreacting. Describing an emotional experience in a way that deconstructs each aspect helps you regulate your emotions when they arise and achieve greater emotional balance.

CHAPTER 4

Validation for Beginners

Validation is a critical communication skill for better relationships. This skill is often misunderstood, so a definition is useful. *Validation* is the confirmation that someone's inner experience is understandable and relevant.

When you validate, you communicate directly and indirectly to another that their experience is important, their thoughts are understandable, or their feelings make sense. Validation can foster *coregulation*, a process that helps you and your loved one process emotions or at least stops them from escalating. Everyone needs to be validated; it usually feels good!

The Benefits of Validating Your Loved One

Validation increases trust and self-confidence. Chronic invalidation of feelings, thoughts, or motivations can leave people not knowing what to believe, what is true, and if the source of information is reliable. A core aspect of BPD is hypervigilance and mistrust of information and new knowledge coming from another person (Duschinsky and Foster 2021). Accepting your loved one's inner experience without judgment rebuilds trust and increases their self-confidence.

Most people who experience frequent emotional dysregulation try hard to avoid or escape painful feelings. Validation sheds light on the emotion without judgment and invites acceptance of feelings. Contrary to what many believe, distress is usually reduced upon being recognized, accepted, and reassured that it is understandable and makes sense.

Emotional arousal will undoubtedly increase if your loved one perceives you are not listening, misunderstanding, denying, ignoring, disbelieving, or judging them. Emotions usually decrease after an interaction based on understanding, connection, deep listening, and presence—in other words, validation.

Validation reduces isolating behaviors because it signals an atmosphere of social support and safety. Being accompanied by an interested, understanding, nonjudgmental person reduces social anxiety and shame.

As you learn to validate others, you will become more centered and grounded because you will be more skillful and less reactive to others' emotional responses, more competent at navigating difficult conversations, and more confident that empathic validation can help you respond effectively.

Validate Only "The Valid"

Have you ever apologized for things that were not your fault, indulged in someone's insistent demands for your time and attention, or agreed to just about everything your loved one said—even when your stomach was in a knot trying to say no? Swept up in fear of your family member's explosive reactions, or just trying to calm them down, you may be "validating the invalid" or accommodating problem behaviors. While understandable, these responses do not help your loved one recognize, accept, and cope with their emotions. They may sustain the expectation that it is your job to accommodate their wants and needs or soothe their emotions when they are distressed. Genuine validation empowers your loved one to solve their problems and helps you realize it is not your job "to make everything all better!" (Lundberg and Lundberg 1995).

What is always valid?

- Emotions and feelings

- Wants, desires, and needs (that may or may not be satisfied, or satisfiable, but they are authentic and understandable)

- Opinions, tastes, and preferences (as long as they are not expressed as facts)

- Good intentions (even if they failed)

What is sometimes valid and sometimes not?

- Thoughts

- Behaviors and actions

- Plans and solutions for problems

What is rarely valid?

- Lies

- Illogical arguments

- Excessive threats or insistent demands

- Screaming, ranting, raging, or insulting

- Violent behavior, such as insults, hitting, or breaking objects

- Exaggerations, black-and-white thinking, generalizations

- Interpretations and opinions stated as facts

When someone is emotionally dysregulated, look for what is valid. Validate that and ignore the other things for the moment (as long as there is no physical violence). In later chapters, you will see how to respond in ways that change behavior, but learning to validate is the first step.

What Validation Is Not

As you begin to understand what validation is and how to begin practicing it, it's important to understand what it is *not*. Even if a response is well received, it's not necessarily validation. Validation is not:

- **Praise.** "You look pretty" is not validation. It could even be invalidating if someone is not feeling that way. (That does not mean that all praise is bad; it is just not validation.)

- **A value judgment.** "You did great" may be received as another heavy-handed opinion, especially from a parent if their son or daughter did not feel they "did great."

- **Consolation.** "You poor thing—what a shame that happened to you. I'll take care of it." This response often reinforces passivity or validates an ineffective or invalid attitude.

- **Saying "I'm sorry."** If you say "I'm sorry," then you are literally describing your feelings. This is not validating. The response may be a blank look or more anger.

- **Saying "I understand."** These words can be perceived as an attempt to stop a person from speaking. If you really understand, you should be able to describe exactly what you understand.

- **Telling another how they feel.** To validate is to offer a hypothesis. "You are angry" could land as invalidating. "That sounds annoying" is more likely to land as validating.

- **Saying "Calm down."** This can increase your loved one's emotional arousal because they cannot just calm down, or they would.

Even worse, you will likely *invalidate* another and escalate an emotionally charged dialogue or conflict if you go into:

- **Problem-solving.** When someone is emotionally activated, suffers from cognitive distortions, or is stuck in black-and-white thoughts, logical reasoning does not work.

- **Explaining yourself.** It is not helpful to describe your reasoning for thinking or doing something, or defend yourself by justifying your behavior or thoughts.

- **Giving advice.** Even with the best intentions and gently offered with kindness, advice is invalidating. It communicates, "I know better than you how to manage your life." That stings! If someone asks for advice, resist a little, ask more questions, and recognize them as intelligent and capable. If they insist that they really want your advice or opinion, be reluctant and describe your ideas from firsthand experience, using statements that start with "I" and not with "you."

A note about encouragement and support: Encouragement and support are rarely validating. They can feel like pressure and invalidate someone's fears. "Come on, you can do it," "You are strong," or "You are smart enough." These are not examples of validation. Depending on the situation, these phrases might feel encouraging at times and not at other times.

It's more effective to encourage someone by reminding them of a fact or achievement. "I remember when you did that last year. It was really hard, and you did it. You made it through. You can do difficult things and solve hard problems."

Another strategy is to describe your beliefs about their strengths and capabilities (including the potential negative in positive terms). For example, "I know how persistent you can be when you want something. I think you will figure this out."

You might try to simply communicate, "I believe in you." (Think about this. How can you expect your loved one to believe in themselves if you don't believe in them?)

The following four steps will help you understand basic validation. Validate your friends, family, neighbors, colleagues, and anyone you contact. There is only one way to become skilled at validating—practice.

Step 1: Be Present and Listen

- Look directly at the other person. Communicate your interest, nonjudgmental acceptance, and curiosity with attention, facial expression, gestures, and posture—without saying a single word.

- Notice their eyes, facial expressions, gestures, and posture.

- Listen to the words, tone of voice, volume, and speed of their words. Is their voice high or low? Are they speaking fast or slow? Is there an occasional pause to inhale or reflect? Pay attention!

- You don't have to be mute. Appropriate sounds can be validating, like: "Uh-huh... uh-huh," "Oooh!" or "Wow!"

- Simple words can validate, such as: "Interesting," "Oh my God!" or "Ouch!"

- Simple questions can validate, like: "What happened?"

When to Lean In: If your loved one tends to be dramatic and impulsive, or their idea of a good dialogue is actually a monologue and they want your undivided attention or they will feel dismissed, then lean forward and look them directly in the eye. This will confirm they have your attention. This posture will reduce potential feelings of being slighted, disinterested, or rejected.

When to Lean Back: If your loved one tends to be avoidant, anxious, or fearful, and looking at them in the eye intensely turns up too much discomfort, then casually lean back and slightly tilt your head to one side. Relax your face, shoulders, and arms. This can help them feel safe, connected, and comfortable. It can also help to raise your eyebrows in a little "eyebrow wag" when you want to communicate interest, wonder, or surprise in a nonthreatening and non-dominant gesture (Lynch 2018). Try it out in the self-reflection that follows.

self-reflection: Body Posture

Look at yourself in the mirror or with your cell phone camera. Relax the forehead, the muscles around the eyes, and the jaw. Gently lift the corners of your mouth as your cheeks float upward. Now, lift your eyebrows and slightly tilt your head to one side. Slowly say the word "interesting" in a warm, gentle voice. Let your eyebrows drop to a neutral, relaxed position. Does that look and feel nonthreatening?

Practice listening fully to another person without saying a word. Nod your head, be interested, and keep your mouth shut for twice as long as you usually would. How did that feel? Can you imagine any benefit from doing this more often?

_____

_____

_____

_____

_____

_____

Step 2: Reflect Back

Describe your understanding of what the other person is saying, without judgment. If you have a hypothesis about the meaning behind what the other is saying, express it with humility and openness to correction.

For example, "This is important for me to understand, and I want to ensure I get it. You are saying... Did I get that right?" Here's another example: "If I understand correctly, what happened was...[describe exactly what your understanding is]."

If you do not understand, ask for clarification. Listen to the answer without interrupting. For example, "Sorry, I'm not following you. This is important to me. Can you describe it again, but slower?"

Reflect back what you understand to confirm that you understand correctly. Find the "grain of truth," then say how much sense it makes or that your loved one is right about x, y, or z—and be very specific. You can validate a valid thought or perspective. The part that makes the most sense is a fact you can agree with or a reasonable assertion, even if it's mixed with emotional judgments. Finding and reflecting back just the grain of truth may expand clear thinking and reduce emotionally distorted thoughts.

◆ *Audrey, Ellen, and Steve*

Ellen called her mother, Audrey, three times and then sent a text message saying she was going to call the police about her adult son, Steve. Audrey saw the missed calls and called back, asking what was happening.

Ellen responded loudly and rapidly, "Steve has been on the phone with his girlfriend for hours! He won't move his car! I can't go to work! He was just laughing at me! I am tired of this; nothing is going right! He should just move out; he's never studying anyway, and he's gonna fail out of college!"

Audrey interrupted her daughter, who seemed to be spiraling out of control. "Ellen, this sounds terrible! I'm a little confused, though." Speaking a little more slowly, she said, "Steve's car is blocking yours, and you can't go to work. Do I understand correctly?"

"Yes, he refuses to move it, and I'm late!"

Audrey continued to speak slowly. "So, if I understand correctly, you are stuck until his car is moved. And he is not cooperating."

"My boss said he'll fire me if I'm late again. We'll lose our health insurance and I won't be able to pay the rent. It's all Steve's fault."

With warmth and concern, Audrey said, "Ellen, I hear that you want to get to work as soon as possible and are worried about getting fired. That's understandable."

"Mom, I can't do this anymore. I'll see if I can squeeze around his car by driving on the neighbor's lawn. If they call the police, he will have to face them." Ellen hung up.

During the brief conversation, Audrey did not question the accuracy of what her daughter said (although she wanted to). She tried to be empathic and calm and avoid sounding judgmental. Audrey did not try to solve Ellen's problem. She just tried to reflect back what Ellen was saying in a way that validated what seemed valid. As a result, Ellen's panic and helplessness went down just enough for her to stop complaining, hang up, and solve her problem. It may not have been an ideal conversation, but it was a lot better than in the past.

exercise: Reflect Back

Think about a recent conversation when your loved one was emotionally aroused. What were they saying? Can you write down two or three sentences that would effectively reflect back what was said?

_____

_____

_____

_____

_____

_____

_____

Step 3: Breathe. Ask Yourself, Am I in a Wise Mind?

This step is technically not validation, but it is fundamental to your ability to validate. If you are anxious or annoyed, validating can be challenging—perhaps impossible. Chances are high that you will make a bad situation worse. Getting into Wise Mind and managing your emotional activation might be as simple as pausing to take a few deep breaths and releasing tension with each exhale.

If a few seconds is not enough, take a "bathroom break" (nobody responds by saying you can't go to the bathroom). You can step into the bathroom, breathe slowly for a few minutes, and splash cold water on your face. (You'll read more about the bathroom break in chapter 7.) If you need even more time to calm down, decide how much you need and say you need a break. Go for a walk. Wait until after dinner. Sleep on it. Just remember to return to the conversation when you say you will. You will be much more effective at validating when you are present, calm, and grounded.

If necessary, validate yourself, perhaps saying to yourself: "My feelings are understandable." "They are authentic and legitimate." "Anyone in my shoes could feel what I'm feeling." You might call a trusted friend. You can also practice mindfulness of your emotions, observing and describing your feelings (see chapter 3).

Step 4: Name the Emotion

What emotion is your loved one experiencing? Name the emotion, being tentative and open to correction. What activated it? It's not necessary to know exactly what caused the emotion, but use the best information you have. Follow these tips to increase the likelihood that naming the emotion will actually land as validating.

Tip 1: Try to attach the emotion to the situation that activated the emotion, not the person who feels the emotion. For example: "That would have been embarrassing," rather than "You must have been embarrassed."

Tip 2: Use words that are "acceptable" in your family or for your loved one. Acceptable words are often more general and less intense. For example, "That sounds uncomfortable," rather than "You must have been dying of shame." Examples of low-intensity emotion words that are attached to the activating situation include:

- "That situation seems like it would be frustrating."

- "It's understandable that it would be annoying!"

- "That sucks!"

- "What disappointing news!"

- "Everything you're going through is overwhelming."

- "That sounds hard!"

- "How uncomfortable that must have been!"

Even with the best intentions, words can escalate emotional arousal. Constructing statements carefully will help prevent denial or defensiveness and increase the chances of the response landing as validating. You can always ask, for example:

- "Do I get it?"

- "Tell me if that resonated with your experience."

- "How stressful was it?"

exercise: Words Matter

Many families have loved ones react to their attempts at emotional validation with defensiveness or denial, such as "I'm not angry!" or "You don't know how I feel!" or "Don't try that mumbo-jumbo with me!" To prevent or reduce these reactions, list what you think are acceptable words for your family member to describe their feelings or beliefs. Make it into an adjective for the activating event.

Check off words you might use to validate. "That situation (or person or place) sounds…"

☐ Annoying	☐ Frustrating
☐ Challenging	☐ Hard
☐ Confusing	☐ Horrible
☐ Difficult	☐ Painful
☐ Disappointing	☐ Scary
☐ Dreadful	☐ Stressful
☐ Embarrassing	☐ Tough
☐ Exhausting	☐ Uncomfortable

Find other words already used by your loved one. For example: She often says she is worried and impatient. He insists that others are disrespectful.

Other words: _____

_____

_____

_____

• *Rina, Joshua, and Jessi*

Joshua wanted his daughter, Jessi, to achieve in school and sports like he did. His parenting had been modeled after his parents' encouragement to succeed. Jessi was in her second year in college but took only three courses while doing DBT therapy. When she told her parents she passed all three exams, her father replied, "Jess, that is the best present you could give me. I am so proud of you. Maybe you can go back to a full load in January." Jess started to cry, went to her room, and slammed the door.

Joshua looked at his wife, Rina, who just glared at him. "What?" he demanded. "I just wanted to encourage her!"

Rina whispered, "You're supposed to validate, not pressure her." Then she got up, knocked on her daughter's door, and entered the room where Jess was sobbing into her pillow.

Rina said, "Jess, I know you worked really hard this semester juggling classes and therapy. You got through the exams, and that was a lot of stress. Now that it's over, you don't need more pressure from your father. I imagine you expected it to be a relief to come home and get some rest, not a disappointment."

Jess stopped crying. After a minute, she said, "You're right. I always expect it to be better." She sat up in bed, and they continued chatting for another half hour.

Rina continued using her best beginner validation skills, listening attentively, reflecting back what she understood, breathing and checking into her Wise Mind, and connecting Jessica's emotions to the activating event as best as possible.

exercise: Change Invalidating Reactions to Validating Responses

Make a list of two invalidating phrases you use frequently, such as "It's not such a big deal" or "Really?" (in a sarcastic tone of voice). Then list three validating phrases you might use to replace them, such as "I can see how important that is for you," "That situation sounds like it was nerve-wracking," or "Can you tell me more?"

List two invalidating phrases you will stop using:

1. _____

2. _____

List three validating phrases you will start using:

1. _____

2. _____

3. _____

Afterward, try the three validating phrases with your loved one and see how they land.

◆ *Phoebe and Daphne*

Phoebe received a text from her daughter, Daphne, blaming her for her aches, pains, and tiredness because her mother "made" her get vaccinated. Phoebe tried to calm Daphne down by sending her this message: Hi Daphne, Sorry to hear you're panicked about the vaccine. Maybe it would help if you stopped listening to conspiracy theories. There are many explanations for feeling exhausted lately. I don't think it's caused by the vaccine. Maybe you should consult a doctor. Again, I'm sorry for everything, and I hope we can move on. Love you!

Daphne responded with the following text: F-you go to hell!!!!

Phoebe was shocked. "Once again, Daphne thinks everything is my fault. I tried to be nice. I apologized even though I don't think I did anything wrong. I didn't hold a gun to her head to make her get vaccinated. I just said that I thought it was a good idea. I don't know if I want to keep trying anymore."

What happened there? Phoebe thought that she could say sorry. Actually, "I'm sorry" is about herself and her own feelings, not about Daphne. Phoebe thought some helpful advice would make Daphne feel better. For Daphne, the advice felt like condescending pity and proof that her mother did not understand or even care about her.

To validate Daphne, Phoebe could have texted: Hi Daphne, With so much out there about vaccines, it can be scary to get vaccinated. Those aches and pains sound exhausting. I can see how it would be annoying that I told you that I thought getting vaccinated was a good idea. Are you able to get some rest today? *Such a message might have helped Daphne accept her discomfort and tended to her needs, instead of escalating blame and distress.*

exercise: Practice Validating

During the week, look for opportunities to practice validation skills. Validate anyone and everyone in your life. Then, choose one time you practiced validating and answer the following questions.

Describe the situation: _____

_____

_____

_____

What exactly did you do or say to your loved one?

_____

_____

What was the result?

_____

_____

Then how did you feel?

_____

_____

Would you do or say something different next time? If yes, describe it.

_____

_____

_____

_____

self-reflection: Self-Validation

Practicing self-validation is extremely important for two reasons. First, the world is an invalidating place and your loved one may direct intense invalidation, blame, and criticism toward you. Second, your head can be an invalidating place! Many of us have an inner critic that generates self-judgmental thoughts, unflattering comparisons, and standards for ourselves that are always out of reach. Recovering from invalidation involves being kind to yourself by using validating thoughts, gestures, and actions. Connect with others who understand your experience and appreciate how hard you are trying. If necessary, teach a good friend to validate you!

Consider this: Perhaps you have tried everything to help your loved one, improve your communication with them, and better your relationship. Do you often feel frustrated, scared, and confused when your loved one overreacts to something you say? It is understandable if you are sad, grieving for a loved one living with so much dysfunction. You might even get frustrated, or even furious, with your loved one's inability to understand your experience in the relationship. It can also be scary not knowing when the next crisis will happen.

Does the previous paragraph validate your feelings, or does it miss the mark? How?

_____

_____

_____

_____

How would it feel to connect with someone who understands your feelings and does not judge or expect you to feel differently? Would that feel validating?

_____

_____

_____

_____

Summary

Validation communicates to another person that their internal experience is understandable and makes sense. It improves communication and relationships, builds trust, and supports emotional regulation. It is a key skill for family members to practice and use as often as possible with their loved one who has BPD symptoms. No communication skill is more important to practice if you are seeking ways to improve that relationship!

As you continue to practice validation, you will get better at it. When things go wrong, and feelings get hurt, or when your loved one is in a crisis that has nothing to do with you, validation is the most powerful tool for repairing the relationship. Self-validation is also a key to your emotional regulation and your ability to remain centered and grounded.

CHAPTER 5

Deepening Validation Practice

Now that you have a basic understanding of validation (and hopefully some practice), we will dive deeper into cultivating these skills from the heart. Validation is not just a set of words, it's the intention to connect, the curiosity to genuinely understand, and the desire to effectively relieve the distress you and your loved one are experiencing. Genuine validation deeply sees, hears, and understands a person's experience or perspective. There are six different ways to cultivate validation skills. With practice, you can learn to respond flexibly and move smoothly among various kinds of validation. If your best attempt does not land well or is misunderstood, go deeper. Try to understand the internal experience of the other, seek a response that precisely validates only the valid, and let go of the urge to solve, correct, or change.

1. Be Mindful of Relationship

Relationship mindfulness is being aware of your relationship with a person (Fruzzetti 2006). Relationship mindfulness is remembering that you love this person and desire their happiness. Don't take the other person for granted; don't judge or criticize them even if they make a mistake (which everyone does); and patiently hold space for the other's feelings and discomfort. If appropriate, use terms of endearment to keep relationship mindfulness present, such as "sweetie," "honey," "handsome," "cutie-pie," or any nickname or endearment you may have used at some time. Be present, actively and openly listening with your eyes, ears, and heart.

exercise: Practice Relationship Mindfulness

Over the next few days, focus on relationship mindfulness when you are around your difficult loved one (or anyone else in your family, for that matter!). Take your time and afterward answer the following questions.

What did you do?

☐   Remembered this is a person I love.

☐   Remembered that I want this person to be happy.

☐   Used these terms of endearment: _____

☐   Was present with my eyes and ears and heart, listening to my loved one talk.

☐   Other: _____

Did you notice any changes in your communication with this practice?

_____

_____

_____

_____

_____

Did you notice any changes within yourself?

_____

_____

_____

_____

_____

2. Inquire with Wonder

Wonder is an attitude of inquiry that is deep and open, without having all the answers. Wonder frees your mind of preconceived judgments and negativity. It stops you from pretending to understand or assuming that you get it. Wonder can lead to more joy in your relationships and life. If you can hold your inner experience and your loved one's inner experience within a state of wonder, validating questions and reflection naturally arise.

To cultivate wonder, start with a beginner's mind as if this is the first time you have ever had this conversation or this experience, which is true. Gently and tentatively ask questions with nonjudgmental curiosity.

• *Ana and Andy*

Ana and Andy had been living together for two years. Their relationship was having problems. Andy often felt annoyed and angry, which activated Ana's anxiety. Ana felt she would never make him happy. Ana tried validation, inquiring with wonder and curiosity. She made a conscious effort to ask questions and reflect back the answers as much as possible in a warm and friendly tone. Here's an example.

Ana: *Andy, we have had a lot of conflict lately. I'm wondering how you feel about our relationship.*

Andy: *Well, you never pay attention, you're addicted to your phone, and you don't take me into account.*

Ana: *So you feel I am doing things that bother you, and I don't take you into account? Wow, interesting.* [Silence.]

Andy: *Like the other day when you left the trash bag by the back door, and when I opened the door, it fell over. You don't pay attention and you don't think about me.*

Ana: *You opened the door and it hit the trash bag? I didn't know that. What did you do?*

Andy: *I had to pick up the things that fell out. You can't leave the bag there.*

Ana: *Okay. Can we go there so I can understand what happened, and we can figure out how to avoid that from happening again? Would that be okay with you?*

Andy: *Sure.*

Ana avoided entering into an argument and even disarmed Andy's annoyance with an attitude of interest and curiosity. She did not defend herself; instead, she asked about his experience and reflected back her understanding. That may seem like a lot of effort. But would you rather take an extra two minutes to patiently inquire or quickly end up in an emotionally dysregulated power struggle?

exercise: Cultivate and Apply Wonder to Validate Your Loved One

When your loved one is nearby where you can see them, pause and take a metaphorical step back. Observe your loved one as an amazing human being in front of you. Be curious about what it's like to be behind their eyes, between their ears, and inside their skin in the moment. Quietly observing the other, what do you think this person feels, wants, or needs? What's motivating their behavior?

After a few moments of observing with wonder, ask your loved one a question, any question, from this place of curiosity. Listen to their answer, then reflect what you heard back to them, if appropriate. Check to see if you understood the other's response accurately. Be open to correction and revision from them. This may result in a back-and-forth as you get closer and closer to clarifying what the other is communicating.

What happened? How did that go? Is there anything that you would say or do differently next time?

_____

_____

_____

_____

_____

_____

3. Read Minds with Empathy

Empathy includes awareness of both our common humanity and our separateness. It's essential for validating emotions. You can use it to validate your loved one more accurately.

Some people describe empathy as mind reading. However, it's more accurate to call it "body reading" as you read your *own* body! Upon observing another person, the mirror neurons in your brain are automatically activated, and they send signals to your body. Listen to those signals to put yourself in the shoes of another, imagining what they would see, hear, and feel. Empathy involves experiential resonance with another person. It is having the sense of *I know what you are feeling because I have felt that too.* Separateness and groundedness are necessary because empathy does not confuse another person's feelings with your own.

Validating with Empathy

Do you wish you could name the "elephant in the room"? An emotion can seem that big! It can underlie thoughts, problems, denials, and distractions. Often, exposing the elephant results in threats, blame, or other verbal explosions, so nobody talks about it.

Validating with empathy often involves this emotional elephant. To validate another's emotion, you might have to explore. It's helpful to let go of the content of their words and pay more attention to their emotion. Following the details of a story, explaining yourself, and offering solutions can move you away from seeing the emotion, toward invalidation. Instead, pay closer attention to your loved one's tone of voice, speed of words, facial expression, and gestures. Try doing this when their emotion is subtle. See if you can catch a change in the "temperature" of what the other is saying or doing. Then you can ask, for example, "What just happened there? I heard your voice change."

Name the emotion in a kind, supportive, nonjudgmental way, as if it were a concrete observation. For example, "It seems to me that you are worried about it." Or "I hear the sadness in your voice. Is something bothering you?" Notice that these observations do not begin with "you" (as in "You look sad,") which might set off more emotional dysregulation. You are sharing your observation about the other's feelings, not telling them what they feel.

Empathic validation does not always have a sweet and tender tone of voice. The energy has to move in the direction of the other person's emotion. If a person is sad, then speaking slowly in a soft, warm voice may be helpful. If someone is raging, then speaking in a louder, more emphatic tone helps. A bit of animated surprise in the voice will be more effective because it will feel more genuine. Here are some examples.

To validate more intense anger, use a stronger tone of voice:

- "How infuriating that must be!"

- "You must have been pissed off when that happened!"

- "I get it. You are angry."

- "Wow, anyone would be resentful in that situation."

To validate less intense anger, use a relatively calm tone of voice:

- "That sounds annoying."

- "I imagine you are feeling frustrated now."

Do not expect that one validating comment will make someone's anger disappear. If you validate and the emotional temperature does not climb even further, you are on the right track.

If your loved one pauses in response to your validation, let it be. Hold the silence. Do not respond. Breathe. Do not throw another log on the fire. Silence might indicate that some of the emotional energy has been released or that they are reflecting on what you said. Be patient.

When Anger Is Directed at You

The biggest validation challenge is when your loved one is angry with you. In this case, focus on the emotion and let go of the natural tendency to defend yourself or logically explain anything. Talking about your perspective will likely escalate the emotional dysregulation. Do your best to validate the emotion with presence, wonder, and empathy—ignoring the specifics of their accusation.

◆ *Aisha and Rohan*

Aisha and Rohan were married for twelve years, and her language had become very aggressive. Rohan was learning how to validate her.

Aisha: *I have lost all respect for you. You are the worst husband in the world!*

Rohan: [Taking a deep breath, looking wide-eyed, and speaking with heartfelt emphasis.] *It must be horrible to feel like you have the worst husband in the world.*

Aisha paused. She did not know what to say. "It is," she responded and left the room. Rohan was shocked. It felt like it was the first time he had ever disarmed her criticism.

When you are verbally attacked, breathe. Try to see your loved one's emotional dysregulation. Do not buy into the cognitive distortions. Self-regulation may require extra courage, nonjudgment, and a big dose of acceptance.

◆ Pablo and Carina

These siblings worked together in a family-owned firm. Pablo was easily frustrated and often criticized his sister.

Pablo: *Nobody wants to work with you. Tomas doesn't want to work with you. Julia doesn't want to work with you.*

Carina: [She was surprised, confused, and hurt. It took her a minute to collect herself and validate, instead of defending herself or attacking her brother.] *"It sounds like I did something that offended you."* [Expressing genuine surprise in her facial expression.] *"Is there something you want or need from me?* [Her vocal tone communicates open curiosity.]

Carina continued to explore Pablo's feelings, wants, and needs without defending herself and without trying to solve the situation. She disarmed his frustration after a few minutes.

If you try to validate a few times and the attacks are not reduced, leave the scene. Validation is not the only communication strategy, just the one focused on in this chapter. You need enough time for emotional agitation to go down. If necessary, take a break for a few minutes, hours, or a day. Separate yourself with a locked door or leave the premises. Validation does not mean that you continue to validate endlessly while you are experiencing verbal attacks or physical abuse.

4. Act Compassionately

Sooner or later, there will be moments when validating only with words simply does not quench your loved one's pain. Instead, "it slips through your soul as through a sieve" (Bernanos 2002). Eventually, you will want to validate with acts of compassion! While empathy is a feeling of emotional resonance, *compassion* is an urge or motivation to act with kindness to reduce or protect someone from suffering. It may be giving a hand when someone needs it, relieving pain when it is present, protecting someone from threat or danger, providing other desperately needed resources, or assisting with solving problems. It might be asking someone if they need a hug and making it a long one. These responses are what Linehan refers to as "functional validation." Compassion is not as much a set of words as it is an action. It seeks to relieve suffering in ways that clearly validate a person's feelings, desires, or needs.

Compassionate actions are not impulsive, nor driven by anxiety. Compassion requires the stability of mindfulness to hold the space for your own feelings and remain centered and grounded while experiencing a loving urge to reduce pain and suffering in another.

Validating with Compassion by Taking Action

If a person is hungry, you give them food. If a person is sad and lonely, you offer a hug and companionship. This compassionate action communicates that a person's feelings, wants, or needs matter.

Upon seeing your loved one suffering, you might ask, "How can I help?" or "What do you need?" Acting as a sounding board might be as much as you can do. Or you might be able to do more to help, be of service, or provide resources for their long-term well-being. Remember, prioritizing short-term benefits over long-term needs or responding to reduce your anxiety or guilt is rarely an act of compassion.

self-reflection: Spontaneous Compassion or Impulsivity?

Think of a time when you felt an urge to do something to help. Was the urge to act arising from anxiety or impatience?

Circle: **Yes**   **Maybe**   **No**

Did you respond to a desire for your loved one's instant relief now, disregarding their continued or increased suffering later due to your actions?

Circle: **Yes**   **Maybe**   **No**

Did you implement a seemingly excellent solution to a chronic problem and expect your loved one to fall in line and sustain some new behavior without evidence they can do that?

Circle: **Yes**   **Maybe**   **No**

Were you accommodating or rewarding dysfunctional behaviors with an act of compassion?

Circle: **Yes**   **Maybe**   **No**

If you answered "yes" or even "maybe" to any of the above questions, you might have responded impulsively instead of with loving compassion. Perhaps it would be useful to give more thought to your actions, anchor yourself firmly in your Wise Mind, or check in with someone knowledgeable and experienced in such situations.

5. Integrate Wisdom

Our ability to validate another person diminishes when we are under stress or in an emotional state. Our minds become agitated, and our thinking can be hijacked. We can become caught up in a vicious cycle of negativity.

If that sounds familiar to you, mindfulness practices will help to get you out of Emotional Mind and into Wise Mind, a place where you see the world from a more balanced perspective.

From your Wise Mind, you can observe how change is constant. Events and experiences all arise, pass, and create conditions for another event. Patiently and mindfully being present in real time cultivates more of this wisdom. It becomes clearer and clearer that everything you experience is temporary and has a cause (or a antecedent) and a consequence. Obviously, this is not unique to you. It is a universally shared human experience.

Validating with Wisdom

Validation applies the wisdom that:

Everything has a cause: You can see how your loved one's reaction has a cause.

Human experience is universal: Your loved one is not the only person to have this kind of experience.

Practice validating with this wisdom. Beth is scared to tell her husband that she wants to apply for a job and work outside of the house. She knows that he wants her to stay home. How can you validate Beth?

Everything has a cause: "Of course you are scared to disagree with him. He has criticized and verbally attacked you for disagreeing with him for years."

Human experience is universal: "Conflict and disagreements in families can be painful. It is totally understandable that you would want to avoid that."

Jim is a shy adolescent who has not left the house alone since a robbery at a nearby pharmacy a few weeks prior. How could wisdom help you validate Jim?

Everything has a cause: "It can be scary walking in the street, knowing that someone was robbed a few weeks ago."

Human experience is universal: "It can feel insecure walking alone in public."

Frank is twenty-seven, and with limited financial resources, he barely makes ends meet. It gets worse when he goes out to a local bar, drinks with his friends, and spends more and more with each round. Imagine that Frank was complaining about not having enough money to pay his rent. It would be very tempting to tell him to stop spending money at the bar. Could you approach Frank from Wise Mind, validate the "grain of truth," and ignore the urge to give advice?

Everything has a cause: "Financial stress and worry can send anyone to a bar for a drink with friends—even if it bites you in the butt the next day!"

Human experience is universal: "It's understandable that you want to hang out with friends and have a few drinks even if there's not enough money to get to the end of the month."

You might have a lot more you would want to say to Frank, Jim, or Beth. Validation is not the only response to use, but it is a start. In chapter 8, you will learn how to say more difficult things in ways that prevent conflict.

exercise: Validate with Wise Mind

Think back to a recent difficult situation with your family member and answer the following questions. You can complete this for multiple scenarios to gain insight into the patterns you and your loved one engage in. Download this worksheet from the free tools website to practice these skills again.

What happened? Describe the situation.

_____

_____

_____

_____

_____

What about your family member's history contributed to their reaction, or perhaps what made them vulnerable?

_____

_____

_____

_____

What activated their reaction to this situation?

_____

_____

_____

_____

What is common, even universal, about this experience?

_____

_____

_____

_____

When have you experienced something like this and how did that feel?

_____

_____

_____

_____

Write two validating statements based on causes (antecedents) and two validation statements based upon the universal nature of the experience.

_____

_____

_____

_____

_____

_____

_____

6. Equalize with Respect

Respecting your loved one as an equal might be hard. You may believe that your loved one has so much immaturity and dysfunction that equality is hard to see. Consider how, despite your different strengths and weaknesses, you both want to be happy and deserve love, kindness, and respect. Your loved one may not be skillful at doing things that cultivate happiness. A person may find relief from one type of suffering when they do something that causes another. (For example, head-banging hurts, but it may temporarily relieve the emotional pain of despair, anguish, or shame.) You might try to respectfully see your loved one struggling to find their own path and desperately wanting to build their own life, in their own way. Just like you, your loved one wants to feel safe and secure, be happy and content, and live free from physical and mental suffering.

exercise: Cultivating Respect

Close your eyes and reflect upon your loved one for a few minutes. Remember things that were difficult, situations that went wrong, or mistakes they made. Imagine what led up to that, how they felt, what they wanted and needed at the time. Now, think about their strengths and talents.

What characteristics can you admire?

_____

_____

_____

How might these strengths shine forth and get them through difficult times?

_____

_____

_____

_____

_____

How might one of their weaknesses also help as they compensate for it?

_____

_____

_____

_____

_____

_____

Validating with Respect by Treating Them as an Equal

Focus on your loved one's competencies. Listen to their complaints, criticisms, or blame, and do not fragilize them. Instead, treat them as competent and ask:

- "What are you thinking of doing about it?"

- "That sounds tough. How are you going to get through it?"

- "It's hard, and I know you can figure it out because you have done so in the past."

Respectfully validating may go beyond validation of someone's inner experience and into encouragement and support ("You can do it" or "I believe in you"). It circles back to validation when concrete evidence is provided ("You got through it last year"). Your message is essentially, "It is hard, and you have done hard things."

Respect can also be communicated by asking for advice. If you can find a way to ask your loved one for their opinion or advice, it's likely to be received as extremely validating. When a close family member says, "I don't know what to do in this situation. Can you give me some advice?" many people light up. If your loved one has DBT skills training, ask them if they know of a skill that would help you and if they would be willing to teach it to you!

◆ *Phoebe and Daphne*

Daphne sent yet another self-deprecating text message to her mother, Phoebe. "My kids are always yelling at me and refusing to help out around the house. They hate me. I can't take this anymore. I am embarrassed to be their mother. I am so sorry. I have literally ruined their lives."

Phoebe responded by validating with respect. "It's really hard to be a single mom, and you are doing an amazing job. Your kids are honest, they get good grades, and they are involved in after-school clubs with their friends. Did something just happen?"

exercise: Write a Validating Letter

Recall a situation in which your loved one was emotionally aroused. It may be a situation that happened years ago and memories continue to retrigger emotional arousal, or it may be a recent situation in which the emotional arousal was not strong.

Write a validating letter (or prepare a validating speech) to your loved one. Find ways to validate the feelings (and beliefs, desires, or actions that are valid). For now, let pass the invalid things they said or did.

Do not use this letter to talk about your feelings. Do not defend yourself or justify past mistakes. Do not expect reciprocity or forgiveness in response to your letter.

It is not necessary to use all of the following ways to validate. Try to use at least two or three.

1. Mindfulness of the Relationship (Listen and observe)

2. Wonder (Ask and reflect back without judgment)

3. Empathy (Recognize feelings and name them)

4. Compassion (Ask what the other needs and offer help)

5. Wisdom (Recognize causes to explain an emotional response or note how a feeling is universal)

6. Respect (Communicate equality and presume competence in your loved one)

After validating, you may close with a question or describe your feelings. The purpose of this exercise is to practice validation. *Just validate*. No cheerleading. No love letters. No praise. Just validate. This does not mean we can never use another strategy, but let's save that for later.

_____

_____

_____

Summary

Genuine validation arises from within. It's not just a set of words. There are many different ways to validate. Nurturing the underlying attitudes and viewpoints will give you the courage and insight to validate repeatedly, even when things go wrong. It is likely that these already connect with your most deeply held values.

Validation has many facets. If your response is not received as validating, communicate with even deeper sincerity that you want to understand and are trying to do your best. Gently serve up another validation. Keep practicing.

If your attempts at validating are failing or if criticism and complaints continue to rain down upon you nonstop, it might be time to move to the behavioral change strategies described in the next two chapters.

CHAPTER 6

Understanding Behavior

Why does your loved one engage in self-sabotaging behaviors even when the consequences are disastrous? Perhaps you want to know how you can seem to get sucked into bad habits over time? How can anyone stop themselves from responding in the same ineffective way again and again?

Let's start by observing what motivates you and how you can change your behavior (the only behavior you have any hope of really controlling). A behavioral chain analysis is a detailed description of what happened before, during, and after a target behavior to understand what triggered the target behavior; what the immediate consequences were; and what link in the chain might be modified to change the outcome. It is a useful tool for understanding why you repeat problematic behaviors and habits, and how to avoid going down the same path again. Practicing behavioral chain analyses will help you manage yourself more effectively and gain more insight into the behavior of others.

Behavioral Chain Analysis

A behavioral chain analysis focuses on a single event, describing precisely what happened, step-by-step or link-by-link, without judgment and criticism. Generalizations about what "usually" happens are unsuitable for conducting a chain analysis. It's difficult to remember all the details of a specific event and it's impossible to know exactly what happened if a story is created from a combination of memories about various events, none of which were the same.

Problem Behavior: This is the behavior you want to change. It should be very specific, such as "giving advice to my son" or "yelling." If you feel your problem behavior is "being impatient with my mother," that is not a very specific behavior. Is the problem that you insist too often for her to hurry up, raise your voice, frequently correct her, or all of the above?

Episode to Analyze: After choosing a behavior to change, identify a specific occurrence when that behavior last appeared. It's useful to do this with a beginner's mind, an attitude of curiosity without any preconceived ideas.

Vulnerabilities: Vulnerabilities can include hunger, overtiredness, stress and tenseness, lack of sleep, recent conflict, or grieving over an unrelated loss. Hormonal changes around menstruation, physical illness, and excessive worrying about other problems are other examples of vulnerabilities. These can all increase your sensitivity to being triggered.

Situational Antecedents: This is a description of the situation and events that preceded the activating event.

Activating Event: The activating event is sometimes the hardest link to identify. It occurs immediately before the target behavior and is responsible for provoking it. Were it not for the activating event, the behavior would not have happened at the moment it did.

Thoughts and Feelings: Often thoughts or feelings about the activating event directly affect the problem behavior.

Consequences: When analyzing problem behavior, immediate consequences are positive or offer relief. This behavior would not be repeated if there were nothing positive that occurred as soon as the behavior began or immediately afterward. Medium or long-term consequences are usually negative.

Look for positive consequences that begin almost as soon as the behavior begins. This is what sustains the behavior even if the short-, medium-, and long-term consequences are quite negative. Consider, for example, how upon starting to yell, there might be a release of tension and a belief that you will get your way (positive), but a few seconds afterward, shame and guilt arise (negative).

Serena and Cedric

Serena believed she was often sarcastic and wanted to change that behavior. After responding sarcastically to her husband, Cedric, in the presence of her mother-in-law, she decided to do a chain analysis. This is what she wrote:

Problem Behavior: *Responding to Cedric sarcastically.*

Episode to Analyze: *Family dinner at mother-in-law's house with five other relatives from out of town.*

Vulnerabilities: *I was anxious in the car. I tend to feel insecure around my mother-in-law.*

Situational Antecedents: *I rushed to prepare the dessert we were bringing and then rushed to get ready. When we were supposed to leave the house, Cedric wanted to finish watching the football game, and I got impatient. We left a half-hour later than planned. In the car, Cedric gave me the silent treatment while I tried to make casual conversation. When we arrived at my mother-in-law's house for dinner, I said to her, "Sorry we're a little late. Cedric wanted to watch the end of the game."*

Provoking Event: *Cedric said to his mother that I was always criticizing him.*

Thoughts: *I work so hard. He never appreciates me.*

Feelings: *Hurt and angry.*

Impulsive Behavior: *In front of Cedric's mother, I said, "Oh, so now I'm the critic in the family? Yeah, right."*

Immediate Consequences: *Brief sense of satisfaction and superiority.*

Medium- and Long-Term Consequences: *Guilt and embarrassment for getting hooked and saying that in front of his mother.*

Upon reviewing the chain analysis, Serena felt she had greater awareness of her sarcastic reply and might be able to control the urge in the future.

exercise: Chain Analysis

Identify a problematic behavior or bad habit you would like to eliminate. Carefully think about the most recent time you engaged in this behavior. Use the following guide to describe the chain of events. (The items are listed chronologically, but feel free to complete them out of order, starting with the easiest links to identify or remember.) To do your chain analysis repeatedly, you can download this worksheet online with the available free tools for this book.

Problem Behavior: _____

Episode to Analyze: _____

_____

_____

Vulnerabilities: _____

_____

_____

Situational Antecedents: _____

_____

_____

Provoking Event: _____

_____

_____

Thoughts: _____

_____

_____

Feelings: _____

_____

_____

Impulsive Problematic Behavior: _____

_____

_____

Immediate Consequences: _____

_____

_____

Long-Term Consequences: _____

_____

_____

Solution Analysis

Writing down a chain analysis increases awareness of the problem, but that may not be enough to change behavior. A solution analysis considers what links in the chain might be modified to prevent the problem behavior in the future. Changing only one link can avoid the problematic behavior or prevent it from occurring. If it occurs again, then you should complete another chain analysis of the new occurrence.

Serena reviewed her chain analysis, and she thought of two possible links that she might try to modify: reducing her vulnerabilities and reconsidering her thoughts. She decided to:

- Manage her vulnerability by relaxing and listening to calm music that reduces her anxiety when Cedric stonewalls her in the car.

- Reconsider her thoughts and beliefs about Cedric's comment. Saying she "always criticized" him was an exaggerated generalization from his Emotional Mind. She saw it more as his problem and she did not have to take it personally. With that perspective, she felt she could breathe deeply instead of reacting sarcastically.

exercise: Solution Analysis

To resolve your problematic behavior, look back at your behavioral analysis and explore how to modify the chain of events that led up to the behavior and, perhaps, rewarded the behavior.

What, if anything, can you do to reduce vulnerability?

_____

_____

_____

_____

How might you change or avoid the activating event?

_____

_____

_____

_____

Are there any interpretations or patterns of thought that you can change? How?

_____

_____

_____

_____

Do you need to change your feelings? How might you develop more effective emotional regulation skills?

_____

_____

_____

_____

Can you modify any of the consequences? How?

_____

_____

_____

_____

Given what you have just learned about your behavior, how can you help your loved one have greater awareness and understanding of their behavior? You could inquire and get more information for a chain analysis. You might describe how you gained insight from your chain analysis. Or you might have a reasonable hypothesis about the chain of events behind their behavior and ask them if the potential target behavior is problematic for them.

Summary

Your loved one's behaviors may be confusing and painful for both of you. Impulsively acting out, difficulty taking action, or disorganized and self-destructive behaviors can affect everyone in the family. You may find yourself reacting in ways that you regret, including reacting impulsively or holding yourself back from acting.

A behavioral chain analysis guides awareness, understanding, and a roadmap for consciously choosing how to act. The links in the chain include vulnerabilities, situational events, the activating event, thoughts and feelings about the activating event, the problematic behavior, and the consequences. You do not have to change every link in a chain of events to change the outcome. You only need to modify one link. The behavioral chain analysis is a tool to manage your behavior effectively in order to have a positive influence on your relationships, without any expectation of controlling other people's behaviors. The focus is on you; after all, your behavior is the only one that you have any real control over.

CHAPTER 7

The Science of Behavioral Change

It may seem obvious that, despite your loved one's accusations, it is not "all your fault" that your spouse can't keep a job or your adult child was kicked out of college, for example. Indeed, the consequences of their behavior may be their responsibility, but did they freely choose every action they took? Does anyone?

Understanding what drives behavior is crucial in behavioral psychology and neuroscience. Research shows that behavior isn't just a reaction to immediate events. Consequences of past actions also shape future behavior. This called *conditioning*. This chapter will discuss how conditioning influences us and how it can be used to reduce problematic behaviors and promote healthy, prosocial behaviors in yourself and your loved one.

Reinforcements Increase Behavior

Unfortunately, you may be responding to your loved one in ways that reward and sustain behaviors you don't want to encourage. Just like a loving and caring parent who gives candy to a toddler to stop a temper tantrum, you may unknowingly reward the wrong behaviors simply because you want some peace!

Reinforcement is a technical word in behavioral psychology that refers to a consequence that increases the likelihood that a behavior will be repeated. There are two kinds of reinforcements: *positive reinforcements* (a pleasant reward) and *relief reinforcements* (the removal or cessation of something unpleasant). Examples of each follow.

In a rage, your loved one blames and criticizes you. You are silent, staring at them, frozen in fear and confusion. Your undivided attention may be a positive reinforcement for the raging, which becomes more frequent and intense.

- You receive many text messages from your loved one throughout the day. You try to respond as much as you can, hoping to calm them down. Every response is a positive reinforcement for texting and their behavior continues.

Behavior increases in frequency when it results in relief from something unpleasant. Here are some examples of relief consequences that increase or sustain behavior.

- You understand you should not reward your loved one's problem behaviors, but you continue giving in to their loud, insistent demands. Upon indulging your loved one, you experience relief from their harassment. That relief is a reinforcement that sustains your indulging.

- Despite knowing that giving advice to your loved one is invalidating and likely to activate an emotional explosion, you continue to offer instruction. Immediately upon suggesting your solution, you experience relief from anxiety, which reinforces this invalidating behavior. You continue giving advice!

A reinforcer for one person will not necessarily be a reinforcer for another. For example, a compliment for getting a task done is pleasant for many people and increases the frequency of completing tasks. In other people, praise is experienced with embarrassment and discomfort, and has the opposite effect. Other examples of positive reinforcements that may increase desirable behavior include:

- Pay full attention when your loved one speaks calmly instead of only paying attention when they shout.

- Respond with admiration and respect when your loved one gives an honest and insightful explanation. Communicate appreciation for their clarity, honesty, or insight.

- Say yes to a request when asked respectfully instead of giving in only after your loved one raises their voice or threatens you. Increase polite requests by rewarding them, even if they are a little beyond what you want to give.

• *John and Aaron*

John was concerned about several problems with his son, Aaron. Aaron dropped out of college, slept during the day, played video games on the computer all night, and rarely ate meals with the family. Although John wanted many changes, he chose one behavior: having Aaron share more dinners with the family.

John was prepared to give his son positive reinforcements when he sat down to dinner, after he began eating, and immediately after everyone finished dinner. John planned to thank his son for coming to dinner and discuss things his son might find engaging, like video games and social media. After dinner, he also offered Aaron reinforcements, such as his favorite dessert or playing video games together.

If the frequency of the behavior had not changed, John would have considered other possible rewards. Fortunately, Aaron soon went from eating with them once a week to two or three times a week.

exercise: Increase Positive Behavior

Start with yourself. Write down a positive behavior you would like to increase.

_____

Identify a pleasant or gratifying experience to do afterward to reinforce the desired behavior. (If a natural consequence is enjoyable, mindfully absorb it by observing and describing the positive consequence as it occurs.)

_____

_____

Apply the reinforcer immediately after the behavior, never before. (If too much time passes between the behavior and the consequence, it will be less effective at reinforcing the desired behavior.)

Note or track whether the behavior increases:

_____

_____

_____

_____

_____

_____

Now, identify a behavior that you would like to increase in your loved one. Make sure it is a clear behavior to increase. (This is not always obvious, at first. For example, "not eating cookies" means you want to decrease the behavior of eating cookies, but "eating more vegetables" is behavior you want to increase.) Then write it down.

_____

Write down a pleasant or gratifying consequence you can offer. (Note that natural consequences are the most effective.)

_____

Describe the reinforcers you will apply after the behavior, including: 1) after the behavior begins, 2) during the activity, and 3) after the behavior is completed.

1. _____

2. _____

3. _____

Try it and note how it went. Would you try something different next time? Repeat several times and add additional notes here. You can download this worksheet with other free tools so you can practice these skills on an ongoing basis.

_____

_____

_____

_____

_____

_____

Extinguishing Behavior

If a behavior is frequent, something is reinforcing it. If it's frequent and occurs only in your presence, maybe you are reinforcing it. If it never occurs in your presence, you probably do not have much influence on the behavior. If you want to reduce this behavior, you need to determine what reinforces it. *Extinction* is removing the consequences that are maintaining the behavior.

An extinction plan involves determining what you might be doing that reinforces unwanted behavior and then figuring out how to stop doing it. Start by looking for what happens immediately after the unwanted behavior occurs. Identify the consequence that appears to have a rewarding or relieving effect that may maintain the behavior.

If your loved one engages in problematic or undesirable behavior and you typically respond with attention, think of ways to remove your attention and distance yourself. Some examples might be leaning back and looking away, hanging up the phone, or not responding to a text message.

◆ Rina and Jessi

Jessi politely asked her mother if she could get a new pair of jeans. Rina's first answer was that Jessi already had a dozen. Jessi began to insist. She raised her voice, talked faster, and explained why she urgently needed new jeans. Rina repeated that she had jeans to wear, and Jessi angrily denied it. She started insulting her mother and threatened to cut herself and not go to class the next day because "I don't have anything to wear." Rina felt angry, scared, and exhausted, so she gave in. She handed Jessi a credit card to buy jeans and gave her a spending limit.

What happened here? First, Jessi made a calm and cordial request, and Rina refused it. Then Jessi insisted. At the height of negative behaviors, including insults and threats, Rina gave her daughter what she wanted. Rina rewarded the problematic behaviors that she disliked intensely. After this exchange, the probability that Jessi will engage in these behaviors again, longer and more intensely, increased.

Rina and Jessi both had good intentions for their interaction. Jessi first asked politely but with each explanation of why the answer was "no," she became more activated. The problem for Rina was not that she couldn't say "no." The problem was that she started by saying "no," but then she explained herself instead of validating Jessi, and was unable to regulate her emotions. After Jessi's tantrum and threats, Rina was overwhelmed and agreed to pay for new jeans. This kind of interaction extinguishes a desired behavior (politely asking) and reinforces the undesired behavior (threatening and insulting).

Conditioning is reciprocal. Rina experienced relief from guilt and fear when she agreed to buy jeans. Rina wanted to create a plan to extinguish Jessie's problem behaviors, and she knew it would be complicated. Rina would no longer get the relief reinforcement she (unconsciously) wanted when her daughter yelled at her.

When you do extinction and remove the reinforcer, offering validation simultaneously is often very useful. Validating and extinguishing behavior can be integrated to help your loved one tolerate distress and stop engaging in problematic behaviors. For example, Rina might validate Jessi to avoid a meltdown. She could say, "I understand you want to feel good about yourself in flattering and comfortable clothes. Of course, it's important to feel like you belong. I imagine you would be happy in new jeans. I am not giving you money now, but we can go to the mall in two weeks. If you wait, you can pick out jeans and a top to go with it." This proposal would help prevent escalation and reward patience, which Jessi definitely lacked.

Extinction Bursts

When you remove consequences that maintain problem behavior, it will initially increase! This is called an *extinction burst* and occurs because people expect a reward. The first few times a reward does not appear, the targeted behavior will increase in intensity, duration, or both. Most people who begin an extinction plan intuitively expect extinction bursts. If that's your fear, you are right!

Family members often want to reduce behaviors such as screaming, verbal attacks, profanity, or endless monologues about how their beliefs and actions are all wrong. They don't realize how their presence and undivided attention may reinforce these undesirable behaviors.

Instead of remaining wide-eyed and filled with fear when your loved one is angry and verbally attacking you, try to look away, engage in another task, go to another room, go for a walk, put a locked door between you and your loved one, or even get in the car and drive away. The angry verbal attacks will worsen, so have a safety plan. Involve your extended family, friends, neighbors, or professionals to help you consistently carry out your part of the extinction plan, especially if you believe there is a risk of behavior that threatens life, health, or property. The presence of others may reduce your loved one's acting out. Also, their knowledge of your extinction plan may solidify your commitment to the behavioral changes you are taking on. (If you anticipate an extinction burst may escalate into a crisis, read chapter 10 before implementing your extinction plan.)

The "Bathroom Break" Extinction Plan

If you want to stop verbal attacks but leaving the scene is too scary for you, the bathroom break is a good way to start. Calmly say, "Listen, I really have to go to the bathroom. Give me two minutes. What you are saying is important. I'll be right back." It's hard to argue with that, even if someone is angry at you.

In the bathroom: 1) Splash your face with cold water. 2) Breathe, focusing on long and slow exhales. 3) Look in the mirror and relax your jaw, neck, and shoulders. Give them a squeeze or brief massage if that helps. 4) Shake out your hands and feet. 5) Finally, stretch your neck and arms very gently. Try each to see what's most effective for you. These actions lead to a physiological deactivation of fear in the central nervous system. Upon leaving the bathroom, check to see if your fear is reduced.

If it seems appropriate, say "Hey, I'm thirsty and need to grab some water. Do you want any?" Bring two glasses of cold water, even if they say no, in case they change their mind.

Your loved one has just had to practice tolerating their distress alone for a few minutes. Notice if their agitation has gone down at all. Reward that with your attention, a glass of water, and your gratitude. "Thanks for your patience; I really appreciate it." If your loved one dives back into the argument, try to kick the discussion forward by saying "Can we talk more about this after dinner?". Maybe you could change the subject: "I forgot to ask how your big project has been going."

exercise: The Bathroom Break

Try the bathroom break strategy and reflect on how it went.

Describe the situation.

_____

_____

_____

When you said you had to go to the bathroom, what exactly did you say, what gestures did you use, what was your tone of voice?

_____

_____

_____

What did you do in the bathroom? Check all that apply.

- ☐ Splashed my face with cold water.

- ☐ Focused on my breath with long and slow exhales.

- ☐ Relaxed my jaw, neck, and shoulders.

- ☐ Shook out my hands and feet.

- ☐ Gently stretched my neck and arms.

- ☐ Other: _____

After leaving the bathroom, what did you do?

☐   I got myself a glass of ice water.

☐   I brought my loved one a glass of ice water.

☐   I was able to postpone further discussion of the subject.

☐   I was able to change the subject.

☐   Other: _____

How effective was the practice on a scale of 1 to 5 (1 is not effective and 5 is very effective)?

_____

What might you do differently next time?

_____

_____

_____

_____

_____

_____

Replacing Undesirable Behavior with Desirable Behavior

When you want to decrease a behavior, it is very useful to think about what desired behavior should replace the undesired behavior. You can plan a combination of strategies to extinguish the behavior you want to decrease and reinforce the behavior you want to replace. For example:

- Decrease your loved one's yelling by looking away or distracting yourself; increase their calm tone of voice by responding with warm and kind attention.

- Decrease loud, insistent demands by not giving in; increase polite requests by responding generously.

- Extinguish your own behavior of challenging or advising another person; instead, ask questions with a curious, nonjudgmental tone of voice. Notice and appreciate a positive response from your loved one instead of an emotionally activated response.

Extinction Planning

Due to the explosions of the behavior you want to extinguish, carrying out an extinction plan is *hard*. During this period, it's essential to manage your fear or anger, have support and backup from family and friends for safety and support, and if necessary, seek therapeutic help. Fear may be your biggest obstacle to executing a plan to extinguish a loved one's behavior—especially when you have been reinforcing it for many years.

Faced with the explosion of an unwanted behavior you want to extinguish, you need to combine and integrate several strategies, including reinforcing desirable behavior to replace the problematic behavior and a lot of validation.

Factors outside your control may also reinforce your loved one's behavior. Consuming drugs, for example, offers an immediate positive consequence that you cannot remove. Lying may relieve shame and increase a temporary feeling of superiority. Yelling may provide a temporary relief from helplessness or frustration.

exercise: Planning for Extinction Explosions

What do you want your loved one to stop doing? Describe a behavior you want to extinguish completely.

_____

_____

_____

How do you feel when your loved one does this?

_____

_____

What do you do that might reward or positively reinforce the behavior when your loved one begins to engage in this behavior?

_____

_____

_____

_____

What is the worst thing you imagine might occur if you did not respond as usual?

_____

_____

_____

_____

What is the probability that you think this would really occur?

_____

If the probability is high, what could you do to prevent the worst thing from occurring, and what resources or support would you need?

_____

_____

_____

_____

If the probability is low, what might you do to manage your fear more effectively?

_____

_____

_____

_____

You can download this worksheet with other free tools, so you can practice these skills for multiple behaviors.

The Power (and Problem) of Intermittent Reinforcement

When behavior is reinforced only sometimes, it becomes a well-established habit and is not dependent on being reinforced every time. *Intermittent reinforcement* entrenches behavior over the long term. Shifting to intermittent reinforcement is very important to sustain desirable behavior.

Therefore, if you want to extinguish a behavior, you must remove the positive reinforcers 100 percent of the time, or you are empowering the unwanted behavior with intermittent reinforcement. Many families try to extinguish aversive behaviors, but they end up using intermittent reinforcement. That sustains the dysfunctional behavior and makes it even harder to extinguish.

• *Larry and Carrie*

Remember thirteen-year-old Larry, the Lamborghini? Everyone agreed that his crises were far worse in his mother's presence. Even Larry's psychologist said that Larry appeared to be "acting out" to get her attention.

When Larry started a meltdown, Carrie tried very hard to ignore Larry and to walk away. But inside, she was hypervigilant, scared, and angry when he started running around anxiously, screaming and threatening to break things if something did not go his way.

Sometimes, she engaged with him, trying to understand, explain something, or solve his problem. Other times, she would insist that he jump in the swimming pool to calm down. Occasionally, she gave him medication prescribed by his doctor for such situations. She thought she was ignoring him, but was going back and forth between trying to calm him down and keeping her distance. Larry was getting intermittent reinforcement.

Intermittent reinforcement might explain why Larry's emotional crises were so intense. If he gets attention sometimes and sometimes not, he will continue to escalate his yelling and insulting because, in his experience, it eventually pays off sooner or later.

Remember this lesson: avoid giving positive reinforcement to the behavior you want to reduce or extinguish, and even worse, don't intermittently reinforce it.

Punishment

Another strategy for reducing undesirable behavior is applying punishment. Punishment is a negative consequence that occurs immediately after the behavior and decreases its occurrence in the future.

For example, a mother got a call from her son's school because he was not there. When her son arrived home, she sat down and asked him what happened. He had skipped school to hang out with his friends. She wanted to implement an immediate, short-term consequence. She calmly asked him to hand over his cell phone and said no internet for two days. She planned to arrange for after-school detention for a week, but she was going to leave it to the school to inform him. Punishment is effective when:

- Behaviors are punished, *not* the person. There is no need to shout, belittle, or insult.

- The punishment is a natural negative consequence of the behavior.

- Without a natural negative consequence, the punishment must be clear, precise, and time-limited.

Remember that punishment teaches what should not be done but never teaches what should be done. If you are going to administer punishment, it is important to reinforce appropriate behavior that should replace the problematic behavior. Use validation, even with punishment, to validate the person and convey that you are only punishing behavior.

Relationship Ruptures

For some families, the problem behavior is not acting out but stonewalling or severing the relationship. If your loved one often "ghosts" you or has gone completely no contact, you may be suffering grief and pain for your loss. You may also suffer anxiety, not knowing if or when reconciliation will occur. There may be guilt or shame for having been iced out. Adolescents and young adults have become notorious for "canceling" others from their lives, leaving a wake of hurt and pain behind them. Using reinforcement strategies to change this behavior is rarely effective.

People who tend to cut off relationships when things don't go as expected often have low sensitivity to reward, high sensitivity to threat, and rigid thinking styles. They ignore or minimize positive reinforcements, while negative consequences seem to be everywhere. They may believe it's their responsibility to "teach others" and to "tough it out alone." If you recognize this behavior, try occasionally sending brief validating messages that require no response. With appropriate emojis, your messages may be:

- "Thinking of you. Hope you are having a good day."

- "Hey there, I just felt like sending you warm feelings and thoughts. Take care!"

If a family member is in an intimate relationship and has been pressured to cut you out of their life by an overly controlling partner, look for ways to positively reinforce and sustain any communication channel, even at a minimal and infrequent level. Avoid judgmental comments about the partner. Assume that your communications are not always private.

Estrangement is complex and cuts across many diagnoses. There is no correct response. You may have to stop trying to contact your loved one. Reconciliation, if and when it might occur, is a process that takes time. Repairing a severed relationship goes beyond the focus of this book; however, all these DBT skills for families are useful for navigating and recovering from a temporary or long-term rupture of a relationship. Don't think that your loved one is not suffering. Relationship ruptures are painful for everyone.

exercise: Make a Behavior Change Plan

Identify two of your loved one's behaviors, one very important and one insignificant, that repeatedly occur in your presence that you want to extinguish. Be very specific and describe it without judgment! For example, "Stop being mean to her sister" is not specific behavior. "Stop hitting her sister" is specific behavior.

Important behavior: _____

Insignificant behavior: _____

Select one of these two behaviors that you want to decrease.

Consider how your actions or your response may contribute to sustaining the behavior. In other words, how might your presence, attention, words, or actions reward the behavior?

_____

_____

_____

_____

How will you remove the reinforcing response? (Think of small ways to start. Just looking away, for example, if your attention is reinforcing.)

_____

_____

_____

_____

How will you manage an extinction explosion? How might you validate your loved one to manage it?

_____

_____

_____

_____

Do you need any other resources or support when you remove the reinforcement?

_____

_____

_____

How can you positively reinforce a neutral or desired behavior that should replace the behavior to be extinguished?

_____

_____

_____

Do you need any support to prevent intermittent reinforcements from occurring?

_____

_____

_____

Is there any additional punishment that you think would be useful? If so, what?

_____

_____

_____

Try to put an extinction plan in place with a change in your behavior. Afterward, consider whether you successfully did not reinforce your loved one's behavior. What your loved one does is far less important than whether you changed your behavior. You can download this worksheet along with a host of free tools, so you can create multiple behavior change plans.

◆ *Sara's Extinction Plan*

Sara's father experienced road rage. If Sara was in the car and he missed a turn or something unexpected happened, he yelled at Sara, blaming her because she was the "copilot." Sara yelled back, and it escalated into an ugly screaming match. Sara decided she needed an extinction plan.

Behavior to decrease: *I want my father to stop yelling at me in the car.*

Reinforcements to remove: *My presence and attention are reinforcing his yelling.*

How to remove the reinforcements: *When his voice gets loud, I'll lean closer to the door, look out the side window, and remain quiet.*

How to manage an extinction explosion: *If he escalates, I'll put on headphones.*

Resources or support needed: *Keep headphones in the car.*

Desirable behavior to reinforce: *Be extra attentive and present when my father is cheerful in the car. Communicate my appreciation for his calm demeanor.*

Additional support to prevent intermittent reinforcement: *I sometimes help him with the GPS after he yells, which might result in intermittent reinforcement. I need to control my impulse to help.*

Punishment: *Punishment won't help. I've yelled back many times and it only seemed to make the problem worse.*

Summary

The science of behavior posits that behaviors are acquired through conditioning. A positive consequence increases the likelihood that a behavior will be repeated, while a neutral or negative consequence does not reinforce the behavior. Extinguishing behavior requires determining what you do that reinforces the behavior and then changing your behavior to stop the reinforcement.

Human behavior is complex. Behaviorism offers some strategies for influencing a loved one's problematic behavior by modifying your own responses. If you decide to try reinforcement and extinction strategies, make sure you stay focused on your behavior and how you manage to consistently follow your plan. If you stick to your plan and have correctly identified the reinforcement(s), conditioned learning will occur and new behavior will emerge.

CHAPTER 8

Effective Communication

Often, the hardest part of family relationships with a person who is emotionally vulnerable is not the emotional chaos but the cognitive deficits. Your loved one may be highly intelligent yet have distorted interpretations, selective attention and memory, impaired reasoning, or poor problem-solving skills. If that weren't frustrating enough, your loved one makes instant and absolute conclusions, exaggerates, thinks in black and white, or has a rigid and sometimes self-righteous conviction regarding their point of view. In this state of mind, they may misunderstand what you feel, think, or do—and then be intolerant of your perspective if it differs.

When these cognitive problems invade your relationship, emotional pain and conflict dramatically escalate. Cognitive dysfunction increases even further. Stress and intense emotions can completely hijack your loved one's thought processes.

You may be desperate for communication strategies that fix the problem. If only you could respond in the right way, your loved one would stop the excessive criticism, blame, and anger. Your wishful thinking might be, "If she would just listen to me, she would realize her errors." Such wishful thinking is understandable, but it's actually minimizing the problem and invalidating your loved one. Just listening to you will not make everything better! You have a loved one with some very serious mental and emotional impairments.

You have learned to be mindful and communicate nonjudgmental acceptance with validation. In this chapter, you will learn additional communication strategies oriented toward influencing change that combine with validation to be even more effective.

Intellectual Humility Is a Helpful Attitude

Intellectual humility will help you model more flexible and open forms of communication. This can also help to reduce another person's feelings of insecurity or struggle for power. Intellectual humility is an acceptance of the limits to your knowledge. You understand that mistakes are universal, human, and good learning experiences. There is a genuine willingness to admit your errors, question your assumptions, and value the contributions of others to enrich your understanding. There is an openness to receiving evidence that you are mistaken. Intellectual humility disarms blame, guilt, and the competition to be right. Instead of disagreeing, you can explore other possibilities. Instead of defending yourself, you tentatively seek common ground or shared goals.

Intellectual humility might sound like:

- "I could be wrong about this, and I'm open to hearing other perspectives."

- "That's an interesting point; it makes me reconsider what I thought I knew."

- "I had been thinking of another approach, but I am interested in your insight."

- "Maybe you are right. I certainly don't have all the answers. I wonder if we can look at this together from multiple points of view."

Write two ways that you might communicate with your loved one with intellectual humility.

_____

_____

Amplify Reasonable Thinking

It can be confusing and shocking how your loved one may become swept up in negatively biased interpretations, even in the context of positive experiences. Those positive experiences appear to justify feelings of belonging, safety, or respect, but your family member recalls the event differently. Memory can be affected by selective attention, beliefs, and feelings they had at the time or by the emotions that arose when remembering the event. Cognitive processes may go haywire due to:

- Rejection sensitivity and a fearful expectation of being slighted or dismissed

- Intense worry and hypervigilance to adversity and potential harm

- Sensitivity to differences in interpersonal power and expectations of inequity

- Distrust of incoming information and new knowledge from others (especially from you!)

- Feelings of insecurity and distrust of their own ability to make decisions

If you are tired of the negative interpretations, you probably just want to help your loved one see things from another point of view. Unfortunately, it is highly likely that this will result in a verbal explosion and an end to the conversation.

What can you do? Point out useful thoughts when they arise by validating good reasoning and functional thoughts, if you can find any. Promote and expand functional thinking instead of correcting dysfunctional thinking. Validate and reinforce functional thinking, such as interesting insights, big-picture perspectives, nuanced understandings, and reasonable interpretations when they do arise.

◆ *Denzel, Lashawn, and Sabrina*

Denzel's adult daughter, Lashawn, was a single mother of a teenager, Sabrina. Lashawn often exaggerated or misinterpreted her daughter's comments and called her father in a crisis. One Saturday, she called Denzel, screaming, "Sabrina hates me, and I am done. She just got out of the car, saying she is going to walk home. I bought her sneakers, and she won't get in the car. She's so ungrateful..."

Denzel focused on trying to validate Lashawn, saying, "That sounds like it would be infuriating." He thought of one reasonable and functional behavior. "I know how important it is for you that Sabrina does sports. She needed those sneakers. Lashawn, you are trying so hard to be a good mom, and Sabrina loves sports." He did not have anything else he could think to say, so he stopped there.

Lashawn was silent for a minute. Then, in a calmer tone of voice, she said, "She's standing outside. I'm going to talk to her," and she hung up. Denzel could not control Lashawn's parenting, but he could plant seeds to amplify her reasonable thinking.

Words Matter, So Be Clear and Precise

If you state a judgment or evaluation as a fact, the other person will likely hear criticism and resist your words. When evaluations are expressed as facts, they derail a friendly dialogue with automatic reactions, negative perceptions, judgmental thoughts, and hostile words.

For example, the words *always/never* or *often/rarely* are exaggerations and generalizations that can provoke defensiveness rather than understanding. Accurate descriptions avoid generalizations. The following list illustrates examples of generalizations, exaggerations, or other types of evaluations, followed by clear and precise terms. It really is important to be as precise as possible, even if it takes a few extra words.

- "I didn't invite you because you never want to go," versus, "The last three times I proposed an activity, you told me you didn't want to do it."

- "Please keep me in mind," versus, "Before responding to a weekend invitation, please consult me."

- "I need you to do more around the house," versus, "Could you please set the table before dinner?"

Effect Is Not Intention

How you feel when someone communicates in an emotionally charged manner is not necessarily intentional on their part. This is a common mistake that escalates conflict and hurt feelings for both the speaker and the listener.

By saying, "She is playing the victim," you are mistaking effect for intention. If your loved one describes their suffering or problems and makes you feel guilty, or you believe they are exaggerating, this disdainful expression might conveniently distance yourself from their feelings—as if expressing their suffering were an "act" intended to gain sympathy or help.

You may say, "He tries to manipulate me," about an emotionally reactive person. *Manipulate* is attaining control by unfair or insidious means to serve a personal purpose. People with intense emotions and impulsivity, like your loved one, rarely have this level of skill and control. The word "manipulating" is a negative criticism that can imply something sinister. Consider whether being manipulated has been a behavior that you (unwittingly) rewarded in the past. So, who manipulated whom?

Gaslighting is intentional psychological manipulation designed to cause the victim to question the validity of their thoughts and mental stability, and eventually become dependent upon the perpetrator. This is a rare practice. Interestingly, this word is used by people who are suffering from symptoms of BPD to describe what a family member does just as frequently as families use it to describe their experience of a loved one with BPD.

Your insecure, hypervigilant, and mistrusting loved one could easily feel gaslit when you try to convince them that their understanding of reality is wrong. People with BPD may feel chronically gaslit. Your loved one may tell you that *you* are crazy or lying, with the certainty of knowing the truth. As a result, you feel as if you were being gaslit. However, the other person may just feel angry, scared, and desperate for confirmation that their truth is your reality—when it is not.

◆ *Jack and Marylou*

Jack's wife, Marylou, was demanding a new car. It was not beyond their reach, but Jack wanted to wait until the end of the year. Marylou was alternately crying about how her friends all had new cars and that she was afraid her car might break down. She yelled that she could not be seen in the old car she had. In the middle of this emotional meltdown over a new car, her phone rang. She calmly answered it and went into her bedroom to talk with a girlfriend. She returned ten minutes later and picked up the crying and yelling where she left off. Jack was more shocked by the switch from angry to calm to angry than he was at her desire for a new car. He felt he was being manipulated by her dramatic acting.

Eventually, Jack came to understand that Marylou urgently wanted a new car and was frustrated and ashamed that she was not getting what she wanted and needed. The phone call distracted her and she could control her emotions, speaking to an acquaintance until her attention returned to Jack and her car.

Making Requests and Saying No Effectively

There are many reasons why it might be hard for you to ask for something or deny a request, especially from an emotionally reactive person. Consider the following reasons, identifying whether they are true and in what circumstances.

- **Indecision** is surprisingly common, and you may not realize you feel this way until you try to make a precise request.

- **Confusion** about the facts can occur when a loved one frequently criticizes you, and you begin to wonder what is true.

- **Emotions** interfere. Perhaps your loved one's intense demands, threats, criticism, or complaints activate your fear, anger, or despair. You cannot do or say what you want, including when you committed to yourself and how you would respond.

- **Worries** may stop or discourage you from saying what you want because the other person might get angry.

- **Reinforcements** interfere. You may get a relief reinforcement from giving in and doing what you did not want to do.

- **Skills deficits** are actually very common—you just don't know what to say! You don't know what will work or how to approach the subject, and you don't understand why your loved one reacts poorly.

---

self-reflection: Obstacles to Making a Request or Saying No

Do you suffer from any of the preceding obstacles when it comes to making a request or saying no? Check the obstacles below and note a potential remedy that follows. Then look it up in this book and practice it.

- ☐ **Indecision or Confusion:** Practice connecting with Wise Mind (chapter 2)

- ☐ **Emotion:** Observe and describe your emotion mindfully (chapter 3)

- ☐ **Worry:** Mindfulness (chapter 2)

- ☐ **Reinforcements:** Behavioral chain analysis (chapter 6)

- ☐ **Skills Deficits:** Learn and practice how to make requests (next in this chapter!)

Should the Intensity Be Flexible or Firm?

A request, refusal, or handoff of information may range from indifferent to interested to urgent. It's useful to consider the most appropriate intensity. Some important variables determine the intensity of the communication. These include your relationship with the other person, the amount of give and take, how you feel about yourself, and your influence or authority over your loved one or their authority over you. A range of intensity on a scale of 1 to 5 might look like:

Level 1. Indirect and subtle: While surprisingly common, this is hardly a request at all. It might be perceived as complaining about something, hoping for a fix, or just hinting that you want something.

Level 2. Tentative and openly curious: This is clear, but indirect, communication. It indicates a lack of certainty or hesitancy about asking. The request might not be fully developed, and the other person is not pressured to comply with it.

Level 3. Graceful and flexible: Such communication is direct and open to conversation and negotiation.

Level 4. Confident and firm: Requests, denials, and sharing of information are strong, direct, and leave little space for negotiation.

Level 5. Insistent and rigid: This level of requests or denials may be urgent or something that the other person really has no choice about. It may inform another person about an action that will occur or something that you will or will not do.

Here is a simple example of each level, asking someone to make a sandwich.

Level 1. "I'm hungry!"

Level 2. "How would you feel about making a couple of sandwiches?"

Level 3. "If you are going to make lunch, I would appreciate a sandwich."

Level 4. "I am working against a deadline. Could you please make a sandwich for me?"

Level 5. "It's lunchtime. I can't stop work. I'm starving. I need you to make a sandwich for me."

The level of intensity has nothing to do with the volume of your voice or the speed of your words. All intensities can be asserted in a calm, clear voice and a relaxed body posture.

What Level of Intensity Is Appropriate?

How can you know what is the most effective intensity? Consider using levels 1 to 3 if:

- The person cannot reasonably comply with your request or refusal
- The request or the refusal is not fully appropriate for the relationship
- It's not a good time to ask or to say "no"

Consider the higher intensity of levels 3 to 5 if:

- You know exactly what you want, have checked the facts, and it is important to you
- You give as much as you get in the relationship or if the other owes you a favor
- You have authority over the other person
- Asking will help you feel more confident or have more self-respect

self-reflection: Intensity of Requests or Denials

Think of a request you want to make or a "no" that you have pending to communicate. Write it here.

_____

_____

_____

Review the five levels and the considerations for identifying the most appropriate level. Ask Wise Mind, "What is the most effective level of intensity for me to use for this request (or "no") in this situation?"

Write down the answer: _____

Getting What You Want with DEAR MAN

One of Marsha Linehan's (1993) best-known acronyms, DEAR MAN, represents skillfully structuring a request or saying "no" to others, especially when asking is difficult or the other person may react negatively. This structure is also useful if you are simply informing someone about something when the information is not likely to be well received. Here's how it works:

DEAR: Describe, Express, Assert, Reinforce

1. **Describe:** In one sentence, describe the current situation or the facts about your request or refusal. Keep this concise and precise. Like any good negotiator, start with a point of agreement—just the facts. If you are responding immediately and spontaneously to the other person, this may not be necessary. However, if the other person isn't already thinking about the subject or the facts that are the basis of your request or communication, then describe the facts.

2. **Express:** Express your feelings about the situation you just described. Some people don't like to talk about their feelings, and others note that their loved ones have said they don't care. While that may be true, finding at least one or two words that describe your emotions, physical sensations, hopes, or needs may help the other person understand, empathize, or feel good about complying with your request (or refusal).

3. **Assert:** Assert the request, refusal, or information. Be clear and precise. This is the heart of the whole communication, so make sure you ask for exactly what you want or say no to what you don't want. It can be hard to ask for something directly or to say no, and your loved one may have no idea how hard it is for you.

4. **Reinforce:** Reinforce by telling the person what their reward will be or the positive consequences they will experience after complying with your request or refusal. You want the person to feel good about doing or accepting what you want. Do not forget to provide the reward afterward. If necessary, and there are no real positive rewards for complying, describe the negative effects of not complying.

Now listen and breathe! Then:

MAN: Maintain, Act confident, Negotiate

5. **Maintain:** Maintain your position. If necessary, be a "broken record" by asking, saying no, or repeatedly expressing your needs clearly. Do not respond to attacks. Ignore distractions. Stay focused on the goal. This can take practice if your loved one reacts negatively to what you are saying, jumps into attack mode, or brings up other situations. Do your best to stay on track calmly.

6. **Act confident:** Use a calm tone of voice, relax the body, and make eye contact if speaking in person. Don't stutter, whisper, look at the floor, raise your voice, blame the other, or use profanity.

7. **Negotiate:** Think about possible reductions in the request or alternative requests (or refusals) in advance. Be flexible and open to exploring alternatives. Should you give something in order to get what you want? Negotiate in good faith by asking your loved one if they have another proposal or how they would solve the problem.

Preparing a DEAR MAN is usually harder than it first appears—but it is well worth the effort. Here's an example of a mother using DEAR to say "no" to her son who was insisting for days that he urgently needed another guitar.

"Honey, I understand that you really want a new guitar, and it doesn't matter that you already have two. I'm worried about spending extra money, and I want some time to look at my budget."

Her validating statements are: "The guitar you want is really beautiful, and I am sure it sounds amazing."

She continues: "I am not going to buy it for you. If you can wait until this weekend, I'll have time to look at the numbers. Then we can talk about how you can save up for it, and whether I might be able to help pay a portion."

---

exercise: Practice Writing a Request or Refusal

Think of something that might be difficult to say. You want to ask, say no, or simply inform. Write a script for what you might say if you were facing the person, texting, or emailing, whichever you prefer. Follow the DEAR MAN steps carefully. Remember that it can be done in four short sentences with an additional sentence or two for validation. Try adding the validation before the most difficult line you have, and you will find that the whole communication seems easier and sounds better. Keep it short and concise! The more words you write, the greater the possibility that there will be misinterpretation and emotional reaction from your loved one. *This is a very important exercise, so take your time to compose a letter with four sentences plus one validation.*

_____

_____

_____

_____

_____

_____

_____

_____

_____

_____

_____

Summary

Communication is at the crux of our relationships. The people closest to us are central to our emotional stability or instability. What we say, how we say it, and all the nonverbal ways we communicate are central to how we regulate our own emotions and contribute to the emotional regulation, or dysregulation, of others.

Two people in a conversation can activate each other's emotions and invalidate the other. Your job is to manage your own emotions and how you communicate accurately. You will not "fix" your loved one's communication. Practice using a DEAR MAN again and again. Practice at work, with friends, and with other family members. Practice until it becomes easy. Making requests, saying no, and easily communicating information is a game-changer in all your interpersonal relationships. Do not underestimate the power of a DEAR MAN and validate generously when you use it.

CHAPTER 9

Self-Compassion and Personal Limits

Do you sometimes criticize yourself for overreacting to your loved one? Have you regretted judgmental responses or blamed yourself for trying to give advice (which backfired yet again)? You may get caught up in family drama or over-identify with your loved one's angry words. Perhaps you find yourself repeatedly subordinating your needs and feelings out of fear of your loved one.

If you are stuck in a bad situation, maybe it's time to do something different. Instead of focusing exclusively on helping, fixing, validating, and shaping another person, do a U-turn and attend to yourself. Self-compassion can help bring your life into balance.

Being hard on yourself will likely make you feel inadequate, frustrated, or discouraged. Self-compassion and self-validation help you feel more competent and have a wiser perspective. To determine how self-compassionate you are now, you can download a bonus assessment with the free tools that are available online.

We all find ourselves low on self-compassion at one point or another. When you find yourself engaged in harsh self-talk, it might be useful to try one of the following responses.

- Ask yourself: *If I loved myself, what would I say to myself right now?*

- Notice self-critical thoughts and replace them with kinder language. For example, *I can't do anything right* is harsh, while *I have suffered a lot, so my progress may be slower* is kinder.

- Imagine you're talking to a child who was bullied on their way to school. How would you talk to that child with compassion? You might say, "It's okay. That was not right. I am here for you. I would like to walk beside you." Use this language toward yourself.

- Ask your Wise Mind, *What do I need right now*?

Attending to yourself with warmth and comfort is *not* self-indulgent or selfish. Research shows that professional caregivers such as therapists, nurses, doctors, and clergy who are self-compassionate experience less fatigue and burnout, sleep better at night, are more engaged and fulfilled in their work, and report greater confidence in calmly providing compassionate care to others. Family caregivers who are more self-compassionate experience less distress in their relationship (Neff 2021).

Tender Self-Compassion

Compassion for yourself means being aware of your stress, pain, or tension and providing yourself with the validation, support, and protection that you need. Self-compassion has two faces: tender and fierce. The warm and tender side offers kindness and understanding when things go wrong. Tender self-compassion activates comfort and reassurance directed toward yourself. It has three components: kindness, humanness, and mindfulness.

- **Kindness:** Generate considerate thoughts, understanding words, and kind deeds for yourself based on self-love or self-care instead of disparaging appraisals or high-pressure tactics.

- **Humanness:** Remember that mistakes and failures are part of being human—everyone makes them. You are not alone, nor are you the worst. Like everyone else, you are doing the best you can.

- **Mindfulness:** Accurately observe and describe reality just as it is in the present moment without judgment and with acceptance. This will develop the clarity and emotional balance that prevent you from over-identifying with disappointing or frustrating thoughts, feelings, and events.

Only one person in this world can accompany, validate, care for, and protect you wherever you go for the rest of your life. You are that person, dear reader. Take a few mindful breaths in that spirit and imagine you are exhaling tension and inhaling spaciousness into your body.

exercise: Cultivating Tender Self-Compassion

To practice tender self-compassion, practice "I'm OCAY." The acronym OCAY invites you to Observe, Connect, and Accompany Yourself using words and gestures.

Observe: Sit comfortably in a chair with both feet on the floor and your back straight. Place your palm against your cheek and rest the elbow of that arm in the other hand. Notice the sensations of your palm and your cheek. Gently lean your head into the palm and attend to the sensations of this posture with each breath.

Now, bring to mind a difficult situation. Name it and use words that acknowledge your suffering, such as "My loved one's behavior is really hard for me," "I am so disappointed with how things are right now," or "It is incredibly frustrating." Describe your painful experience and feel your head resting in your hand.

Connect: Now, pick up your head, bring that free hand to the opposite shoulder, and squeeze your shoulder as if you were comforting a friend. If it feels good, turn it into a shoulder and neck massage. Connect with your humanness. Things will not always go the way you want them to. Say to yourself, "This is part of life," or "I am not the only one with this kind of problem." Massage the opposite shoulder if it feels good.

Accompany Yourself: Now, bring both hands to your upper arms and give them a few gentle squeezes. Move your hands down past your elbows to your lower arms and very lightly brush your fingertips along the skin of your lower arms, or continue to massage both forearms. Knowing that all the cells in your body are there to support and protect you, you might say to yourself, "We are all in this together."

Gently squeeze or massage the wrist, palm, and fingers of one hand. Then, out of gratitude, gently massage the wrist, palm, and fingers of the other hand. You might say to yourself, "I have two hands working together for me," or "I'm here for me."

Finally, put both hands over your heart. Close your eyes and repeat silently or aloud, "I love myself," with each exhale for another minute.

Take your time with this exercise. Then respond to the following questions.

What was the difficult situation you initially thought about?

_____

_____

_____

_____

What words or thoughts were useful for you?

_____

_____

_____

_____

What emotions arose with this practice?

_____

_____

_____

_____

For some people, cultivating compassion results in a "backdraft." Like a firefighter opening the door to a room with a fire burning inside, you let the oxygen in, and the hot flames of suffering intensify. Despair might arise. Thoughts might appear, like "Nobody ever treated me this way," or "It's hopeless." If that happens, firefighters step back but continue their work. Similarly, try practicing with smaller situations or for shorter periods of time.

Fierce Self-Compassion

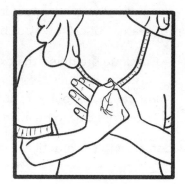

Fierce self-compassion has the feisty energy needed to protect and nurture yourself. You may need to protect yourself from becoming burned out or resentful of your loved one's insistent demands and criticism. You also may need to nurture yourself with active self-care.

If others are overstepping your boundaries, fierce self-compassion will help you to accept and validate your needs, stand tall, and courageously protect your limits. You may have to stop accommodating and limit the time and energy you give to others.

exercise: Self-Compassion with Equanimity

Kristin Neff (2021), a pioneer in the area of self-compassion, developed this practice for caregivers.

Take a few deep breaths to settle into your body. Put your hand over your heart. Visualize your loved one clearly in your mind and notice how you might be stressed, frustrated, worried, or exhausted from this relationship. Notice if there's any stress or tension in your body.

Now, silently repeat several times: "Everyone is on their own life journey. I did not cause this person's suffering, nor can I make it go away, although I wish I could. This is difficult to bear, and I still want to help."

Inhale fully and deeply, drawing compassion into every cell of your body with a loving, connected presence. If you like, imagine your body being filled with white light with each inhale. Let yourself be soothed by inhaling deeply and giving yourself the compassion you need.

As you exhale, imagine you are sending out compassion to your loved one. You can also imagine that as you exhale, their body fills with white light. Continue breathing compassion in and out, allowing your body to gradually find a natural breathing rhythm. Let your body breathe itself: "In for me, out for you."

If you find that you need to attend to yourself and your distress, focus more on breathing in. If you are drawn to attend to the pain of your loved one, focus more on breathing out. You can adjust the strength of your attention as needed, but make sure to always include at least a little focus on yourself and your loved one with each breath. Notice how your body is being soothed and caressed as you breathe.

Continue breathing the oxygen of compassion in and out for as long as you like. To close the practice, silently repeat again: "Everyone is on their own life journey. I did not cause this person's suffering, nor can I make it go away, although I wish I could. This is difficult to bear, and I still want to help."

Upon closing the practice, allow yourself to be exactly as you are in this moment.

Personal Limits

Self-compassion invites you to attend to your own needs and care for them. People with emotional dysregulation are often unable to control their behavior in ways that are considerate of their loved ones (and often not even of themselves!) Observing personal limits was developed to deal fairly with relationship problems that arise from emotional and behavioral instability.

DBT differentiates between "setting boundaries" and "observing personal limits." *Setting boundaries* implies establishing a fixed rule that others are supposed to obey. *Observing personal limits* involves changing your behaviors to protect yourself from the source of frustration, fear, or exhaustion that exceeds your limits. You pay attention to your feelings and take full responsibility for your self-protection.

Sustaining Compliance with Your Limits

Your loved one may often try to push you by arguing the validity of their needs, criticizing you for your shortcomings, or even threatening to run away, leave, or commit suicide. They may talk about cutting and harming themselves or refusing to cooperate until you cooperate with them. They may even call others for help, complaining loudly about your unfair treatment.

Observing your personal limits is an arduous task, especially when you recognize your loved one's intense pain. Protecting your limits and not accommodating your loved one adds even more suffering in the short term, but it moves you and your loved one toward a healthier relationship in the long term. *Sustaining compliance with your personal limits means you must sustain your new behavior, not theirs.*

Limits Too Hard, Too Soft, or Dialectical

Do you believe you are responsible for soothing your loved one when they are emotionally dysregulated? Is it nearly impossible to escape being a punching bag when your loved one is angry? Do you try to fix, prevent, or accommodate your loved one's problems? If you answered yes to any of these questions, you may continually allow your limits to be exceeded. Your limits are probably too soft, and you need to be fiercer with your self-compassion.

Do you believe your loved one will never learn? Do their needs seem so pathological that you have no hope for change? Do you refuse to engage, limit communication, distance yourself, or often avoid your loved one? If you answered yes to any of these questions, your limits are probably too hard, and you may benefit from practicing more tender self-compassion.

Do you easily recognize and accept that you cannot always be responsible for minimizing your loved one's suffering? Do you protect your needs and extinguish your loved one's transgressions to your personal limits with lots of validation? Are you comfortable with extending what you are willing to tolerate and going above and beyond only as necessary? You may already have the flexible limits important for effectively managing a difficult relationship.

Which of these three types of limits do you typically engage in: 1) too soft, 2) too hard, or 3) the dialectical approach, consistent and flexible?

_____

_____

_____

◆ *Francisco and Emma*

Francisco played the violin and needed to practice for two hours every evening at home. His daughter, Emma, would frequently interrupt him for different reasons. He began to notice that his annoyance was affecting his relationship with her. Francisco realized that he really needed that time without interruption. Francisco wrote and rehearsed a DEAR MAN and decided upon a positive reinforcement for complying with his request.

He said, "Emma, I have to practice the violin and I need to concentrate for two hours. I will lock the door to the music room when I practice after dinner. When I'm done, we can have dessert and talk, sing, play, or whatever you want."

Francisco did not ask for her permission nor expect her to agree with him. He described his needs, his new behavior, and a positive consequence for Emma after she tolerated him looking after his needs. After applying the reinforcement a few times, she accommodated his needs. Eventually, he did not have to lock the door.

exercise: What Is Exceeding Your Limits?

Your loved one may test your limits. Remember self-compassion and self-care while you read the behaviors below. Rate those that have crossed your limits on a scale of 1 to 3, as follows.

1 = Only occasionally or rarely crosses my limits with this behavior

2 = Sometimes or moderately crosses my limits with this behavior

3 = Often or severely crosses my limits with this behavior

Obsessive or Demanding Communications

☐   Long phone calls, including endless monologues or frequent emotional crises

☐   Excessive text messaging up to dozens of times per day

☐   Frequent interruptions to conversations

☐   Frequent interruptions at work

☐   Refusing to be alone

☐   Resistance to your doing activities without them

☐   Interference in your friendships

☐   Helplessness, active passivity, or excessive complaining

Aggressive Behavior

☐   Blaming or threatening you

☐   Profanity or yelling

☐   Relentless insistence on demands

☐   Breaking things or destroying property

☐   Reckless driving or road rage

☐   Negligent or aggressive behavior toward a family pet

Occupying private spaces or taking personal items

☐   Entering the bathroom without permission

☐   Leaving personal items in another family member's private areas

☐   Using your clothes, makeup, or other personal items without asking

☐   Stealing money from you

☐   Using your car without asking

Other

☐   Checking your cell phone or computer to read messages, emails, or other personal material

☐   Going through your purse or wallet, closets, or personal spaces

☐   Not cleaning up after themselves or not participating in household responsibilities

☐   Other: _____

☐   Other: _____

Review the behaviors that exceed your personal limits and choose one or two to target for change in an exercise later in this chapter. Unless a behavior is life threatening (always the top priority), choose from the most frequent, most annoying, or maybe easiest personal limit to observe.

◆ *Georgina and Patrick*

Georgina's teenage son, Patrick, stole money or credit cards out of her wallet, usually to order expensive food deliveries. Various punishments had no effect on his behavior and it caused intense conflict between them. Finally, she installed a lock on her bedroom door that opened with her thumbprint, because she might lose a key or forget a combination. Conflict with her son dramatically decreased. Obviously, this did not teach her son to manage his problem behavior (stealing). However, taking responsibility for personal boundaries was immediately effective in this case.

Observing and protecting your personal limits might be clear and direct. However, it is more likely to have to be revisited repeatedly.

How to Observe Your Limits

Clarify your limits. Be precise regarding time, duration, and frequency of behaviors. Then effectively observe your personal limits, step by step, as follows.

Step 1. Monitor your feelings with tender self-compassion. It's difficult to know your limits until they've been crossed. Warning signs would be feelings of anger, anxiety, exhaustion, rejection, discomfort, or a desire to avoid contact with your loved one. Become aware of the situation before you experience high levels of burnout (feeling unmotivated with low energy) or resentment (feeling overloaded, irritable, lacking patience). What situations tend to lead to your limits being crossed?

Step 2. Identify your limits and make a plan with fierce self-compassion. What behavior from your loved one is pushing you over the edge? What bothers you the most and even leaves you feeling resentful? What can *you* do or not do to stop, block, or avoid your loved one's behavior that exceeds your limits? What behavioral change will you make to protect your limits? Will you need support from others and how will you get it? Sharing details of your plan with someone and getting support from another can make the difference between success and failure when it comes to observing your limits.

Step 3. When necessary, be flexible. You may temporarily relax your limits when someone needs more than usual due to specific circumstances. If that occurs, explain the reasons for the change and when you will return to the established limit. If necessary, ask for help discerning whether the situation requires sustaining or temporarily extending the boundary. Check with someone else who understands the situation, if necessary.

Step 4. Communicate how you will change your behavior. Once you have a plan, you may want to communicate how you will change your behavior to observe your personal limits. Honesty about your limits is a way to respect your loved one and treat them as an adult. You only need to communicate this once, so plan it out as best as you can and find the right time. Write what you will say using the DEAR MAN format to inform your loved one how you will attend to your needs. In certain circumstances, you might decide not to discuss your limits in advance; you will just modify your behavior. Trust your Wise Mind to help you decide.

If your loved one does not listen, argues with you, or gets angry, that doesn't mean you did anything wrong. Communicating your limits may activate fear, shame, anger, or disappointment. Try to be consistently firm, especially when your family member does not accept the limits, insists they are unfair, or mocks them. You can agree that it may not feel fair to them and maintain your position.

Step 5. Implement the plan. The easiest limits to implement don't require agreements or negotiation. After informing your loved one, follow through by putting something under lock and key, blocking the incoming text messages, not picking up the phone, or walking away. Observing your personal limits is not about others; it's about you and your behavior.

exercise: Observe and Protect Your Limits

What limit gets pushed, and how do you feel when it happens?

_____

_____

_____

_____

Describe the intolerable conduct that transgresses the limits, including when and where it last occurred.

_____

_____

_____

_____

Is it possible to physically do something to prevent this person from repeating the transgression? (For example, lock the door, turn off the phone, use a lock box, or set up a security camera.)

_____

_____

_____

Write a validation and a DEAR MAN. Cheerlead to request a behavioral change in the other person:

1. Validate the needs, suffering, good intentions, and strengths of your loved one.

_____

_____

_____

2. Describe the situation that exceeds personal limits.

_____

_____

_____

3. Express your feelings (overwhelmed, tired, angry, and so on).

_____

_____

_____

4. Assertively communicate what change you expect or will do to protect your boundaries.

_____

_____

_____

5. Reinforce the positive consequences for the relationship that respecting limits will have.

_____

_____

_____

6. Can you provide other reinforcements when the person complies with the request?

_____

_____

_____

You can download this worksheet with other free tools that are offered online so you can practice these skills on an ongoing basis.

❖ *Marcy and Penelope*

Marcy's daughter, Penelope, could talk for hours, hardly ever paused, and constantly interrupted or just spoke over Marcy. She would ignore any attempts to end the conversation. Marcy had to practice firmly ending a phone conversation. "I understand you still have much to say, and I am sure it is important. I have to close…I can't stay on the phone any longer. We can talk tomorrow." After a few minutes, she said it a little louder, more firmly a second time. Then she added, "I must go now. I love you. Goodbye." Marcy hung up and turned off her phone.

This left Marcy very uncomfortable, but she recognized that she also felt the courage to protect herself. After doing it a few times, her daughter acknowledged Marcy's desire to end the call and said she had to go too and said goodbye. Afterward Marcy texted her daughter a heart emoji to reinforce this new level of cooperation.

Summary

When you are worried, overwhelmed, or stressed, validate your suffering and treat yourself with self-compassion. Tender self-compassion is the combination of mindfulness, humanness, and kindness. Fierce self-compassion harnesses courage and energy to nurture and protect your well-being.

Practicing self-compassion can be a solid basis for observing and protecting your personal limits. Your personal limits are located at the point where empathy is replaced by exhaustion or resentment. It can be difficult to recognize them until they have already been exceeded. Regularly monitor your feelings about your relationship, identify how your limits are being pushed, and consider what you can do to protect yourself from having them transgressed.

CHAPTER 10

Managing Crises and Tolerating Distress

A crisis is an urgent, intensely emotional situation. You probably think that crisis management skills are what your loved one needs, not you! But do you recognize when you are swept up in emotional distress in response to your loved one's crisis? Your fear can be paralyzing. Your anger can turn a crisis into a family trauma that lasts for years. Your tears can trigger the other's shame, anger, or contempt toward you.

Managing crises and tolerating distress is hard to do when a loved one is having an emotional meltdown. They might be threatening you if you don't help and blaming you for their problems if you do. Worse, they might talk about self-harm or wanting to die.

• *Marla and Carolina*

At a mother-daughter vacation, Marla asked her daughter if they could take a selfie. Carolina said that she hated selfies, but Marla cajoled her daughter into agreeing and she took a quick picture.

That evening, Marla walked alone while Carolina stayed in her bedroom at their cottage. When Marla returned, her daughter began, "Y'know, Mom, you are so bossy and controlling. All you care about is yourself. I don't know why I came here. You're mean and selfish, and you've always been mean and selfish."

Marla was confused and automatically began to defend herself. "But I asked if you wanted to go for a walk!"

That seemed to enrage Carolina even more. She screamed, "You see? You never listen to me! You have to listen to me!" She continued yelling at her mother.

Marla stared at her daughter in confused silence, feeling numb as Carolina continued to berate her. If Marla was mentally paralyzed, how could she respond effectively?

If your emotional reaction is so intense that the situation worsens, you need crisis survival skills (Linehan 1993; 2015). Upon realizing and accepting that you are emotionally dysregulated and need fast relief, you need quick go-to skills.

Deactivate Skills

Deactivate intense reactions by physiologically modifying the activity of your central nervous system. This process takes about 5 minutes to be effective, and it may last only 10 to 15 minutes. After that, it must be repeated, or you can go to the skills in the next section.

- **Ice and cold water:** Cold water triggers the "dive response," a physiological response that occurs among all warm-blooded mammals upon diving or falling into cold water. There is a reduction in heart rate and blood pressure to conserve more oxygen in the heart and brain. You can immerse your whole face in a bowl of ice water, splash cold water on your face, take a cold shower, or drink a glass of ice water. (Caution: if you have heart disease or cardiovascular problems, consult your doctor first.)

- **Breathwork:** Focusing on the breath can be very grounding. Making the exhale longer than the inhale deactivates the fight-or-flight system and activates the rest-and-digest system. As you breathe, exhale long and slow. Try counting to 6 or 8 on each exhale while counting to 4 or 5 on each inhale. Continue for 3 to 5 minutes.

- **Exercise:** Intense exercise for a short period of time will increase your heart rate and make you short of breath, exhausting the emotional distress of fight-or-flight or disrupting the freeze response. Try running up the stairs, doing jumping jacks, or dancing.

- **Muscle relaxation:** Let go of tension. Distress, fear, and anger are all forms of tension. Listen to a body-scan meditation. Tense up your muscles and release that tension on an exhale. Do some gentle stretches on a yoga mat. You can also download more ideas to Distract and Soothe with the free tools offered online.

BE STOIC

BE STOIC is an acronym for the following six groups of skills that are also useful for getting through a crisis or tolerating acute stress. Here are descriptions of them. Circle the ones you want to try.

B   Breathe and count if you are intensely distressed. Count from 1 to 5 or count down from 5 to 1 during one long slow breath.

E   Energize your body with movement if you are numb or disconnected. Gently pat your whole body with the palms of your hands, including the head, arms, torso, and legs. Stand up and just shake, dance, jump, tremble. Quickly move your entire body. If it feels silly, that's okay!

S   Stretch or soak if you are tense. Do gentle yoga on the floor, slowly holding stretches for 2 to 3 minutes. Or take a hot bath.

T   Take a break if you are overstimulated or exhausted. Go to a different room, especially the bathroom, where you can splash cold water on your face, or the kitchen to get a glass of water.

O   One thing at a time if you are overwhelmed. Focus your attention on the present moment, just what you are doing or seeing or hearing.

I   Imagine your safe place if you are worried or scared (and there is no real danger to your life or your health). This could be a real or imaginary place. Notice everything around you in your safe place: furniture, light, sounds, and the time of day when it is safest. Imagine having all the protection that you need there. Go into that place when you feel threatened. If your safe place includes a higher power or God to make it feel even safer, include such thoughts and prayers.

C   Cheerlead yourself if you are discouraged or disappointed. Look at yourself in the mirror and give yourself a pep talk. "You can get through this" or "You're doing the best you can." Or use the first person, thinking or saying, "I know it's hard. I have done hard things before. It'll be okay."

• *Marla and Carolina*

Remember Marla, paralyzed and numb with fear and confusion over her daughter's sudden criticism and verbal attacks? At that moment, she noticed she could hardly breathe, and that sensation reminded her to breathe and count. She counted from 1 to 4 on the inhale and from 5 to 10 on the exhale. After a few breaths, she felt more grounded.

Marla told Carolina, "It seems I did something to offend you. If you could give me a minute to use the bathroom, I really want to talk about it." To her absolute astonishment, her daughter paused and let her go without arguing.

In the bathroom, Marla tried to reduce her fear using the four deactivate skills. She splashed her face with cold water, held her breath, and then let out a big sigh. She shook her hands and forearms and silently ran in place for a few seconds. Finally, she closed her eyes and tried to exhale tension from her face, neck, and shoulders.

exercise: Practice the Crisis Survival Skills

Stop reading and try at least three skills from this chapter before going on in this workbook. Record your practice as follows:

Name of skill: _____

What was the prompting event that activated your distress?

_____

_____

_____

_____

Maximum or peak level of distress (on a scale of 1 to 10): _____

How many minutes did you practice the skill? _____

Level of distress after (on a scale of 1 to 10): _____

What would you do differently next time, if anything?

_____

_____

_____

_____

You can download this worksheet with the free tools online so you can track these skills on an ongoing basis.

Distress Tolerance Skills

If your distress is moderate or chronic, try cultivating distress tolerance skills (Linehan 1993; 2015). These are additional skills to employ when negative thoughts, unpleasant emotions, or physical discomfort is at a lower level of intensity and linger or repeatedly return. These skills generally take a little longer but may also last longer. The two groups of distress tolerance skills are "Distract" and "Self-Soothe." You'll find even more practices in the online free tools, which you can download.

Distract

Distracting yourself is a useful and important skill for tolerating distress. It can be a problem if it is the only skill you use. If your loved one is not present with you, but you can't stop the worry or the emotional rollercoaster regarding their situation, these skills may come in handy. You can:

- **Distract with pleasant (or formerly pleasant) activities** by doing something you enjoy. If nothing seems fun or interesting, do something you enjoyed in the past.

- **Distract with opposite actions:** Do something opposite to what you feel like doing or that might arouse an emotion opposite to what you are feeling. For example, when you're sad, try watching a funny movie.

- **Distract with your Rational Mind:** Attend to something that requires reasoning or logical thinking, for example, count, add, or put things in order.

- **Distract by building an imaginary wall:** Mentally set aside your concerns about the situation for a while, on the other side of a wall.

- **Distract with kindness:** Find a way to give back or give others joy.

Self-Soothe

Mindfully savor pleasant experiences. Consider actions that help you to be calm, centered, and grounded.

- **Vision:** Be aware of every image that passes before you without clinging to any of them.

- **Hearing:** You can hear only in the present moment. Listen to music, nature sounds, audiobooks, podcasts, the radio, or play an instrument.

- **Smell:** Fragrances can be surprisingly soothing and carried anywhere. Use your favorite perfume, lotion, or essential oils.

- **Taste:** Savor anything you put in your mouth to eat or drink.

- **Touch:** Get a massage or a hug from someone, rub your neck and shoulder, massage or soak your feet, or apply body oil or skin cream.

- **Movement:** Dance, stretch, swing, run, go for a nature walk or to the gym.

Marla and Carolina

After taking a break to apply cold water and shake out her tension, Marla offered Carolina a glass of ice water and sat down. She asked Carolina, "What did I do to offend you? It was not my intention, so please tell me because I don't know."

Carolina replied, "You know I hate selfies. And I told you that my hair was dirty, and you just insisted. You don't care about anything but yourself."

Marla was honestly surprised. She thought Carolina was mad because she went for a walk alone. "Oh my gosh!" she responded honestly. "I didn't realize that hurt so much. I don't remember that you mentioned your hair, but if you did, then you are right. I was not paying as much attention as I should have."

After that discussion, Marla had a knot in her stomach for hours. Carolina seemed fine, but Marla couldn't stop ruminating. She was tired of the excessive criticism and lack of appreciation or empathy. Looking over her distress tolerance skills, she decided to distract herself by calling a friend (and not talking about this event) and then self-soothe, listening to her favorite podcast with a cup of tea.

exercise: Crisis Survival and Distress Tolerance Skills

Create your own written list for surviving a crisis by selecting at least ten skills to try. Practice when you are *not* in a crisis. Try doing one or two each day. After trying each skill on your list, note how effective it was. Rate how well it helped: 1 = not really, 3 = somewhat, 5 = totally. If none was very effective, go back and pick ten more to try.

Ten skills I will try:

1. _____

2. _____

3. _____

4. _____

5. _____

6. _____

7. _____

8. _____

9. _____

10. _____

Do not skip this exercise. Reading about these skills is insufficient. Experiential learning is critical. After you practice crisis survival and distress tolerance skills, you can speak from personal experience. When your loved one is highly distressed, you can validate their feelings, describe what worked for you when you suffered from intense feelings, and then validate again. For example, "This worked for me, but don't take my word for it. Try it and see if it works for you."

Self-Injury Behaviors

Self-harm is a pervasive problem in BPD, with an estimated 65 to 80 percent of individuals with BPD reporting such behaviors (Andrewes et al. 2019). It includes self-cutting, head-banging, self-pinching, or engaging in any behavior that damages body tissue. Self-injury can function to regulate emotions, relieve pain, reduce dissociation, and increase a sense of agency or control in the immediate or very short term.

If your loved one engages in self-injury, exploring the "function" of self-harming behavior may be helpful. Without judgment and with open curiosity, ask about their experience. If you cannot have this conversation without getting emotionally overwhelmed, practice distress tolerance skills. When the timing is right, you might ask:

- "The last time you cut yourself, do you remember what happened that made you decide to do it?"

- "Did it hurt?"

- "How did you feel after?"

Consider your behaviors around their self-injury. Is it possible that your kind and loving response reinforced unhealthy problematic behavior? Perhaps so, if your response to self-cutting behavior was: "Oh, sweetie, what happened? Let me see. I'll get some bandages and take care of that. We should see if you need stitches. I'll cancel my plans, and we can wait in the emergency room together."

It would be more effective to shift toward a neutral but humane response if your loved one has already self-injured: "You said you cut yourself? There are bandages and stuff in the bathroom. If you need stitches, I'll drop you off at the ER."

Suicidal Behaviors

Many people who are emotionally dysregulated engage in suicidal ideation, associated threats, and suicide attempts. You need to distinguish the difference among various suicidal behaviors to have a useful plan of action to deal with these situations as effectively as possible.

Ideation: This includes thoughts or words in which a person speaks about or thinks life is not worth living anymore. These may be seen as having a continuum of significance:

- Generalized thoughts about death or dying

- Having a wish to be dead

- Thoughts of concrete ways to hurt or kill oneself

- Thoughts of a specific suicide plan, including the conditions and the means to carry it out

Suicidal ideation is thinking that death is a way to end suffering. Ideation may occur without action, or it may be a precursor to suicide attempts. It should be taken seriously and addressed directly.

Associated Threats: These are menacing statements that a person will engage in suicidal behavior if their request is not granted. It may also occur as a form of revenge on a family member for something perceived as unfair.

- "I guess I should just kill myself because you won't help me get an apartment."

- "If you leave, my life is over, so I will just end it."

- "If you don't get here now, you'll be sorry because I will just get in my car and drive it off the cliff."

If a loved one uses suicide as a threat, you might give in to the request because you are afraid or you want to calm them. Giving in to threats of suicide will reinforce this behavior and increase the probability of more threats associated with suicide to control your behavior!

Extending is a response that focuses on the more extreme part of the communication (driving off a cliff) rather than what your loved one wants (for you to leave work to come home). An example response is: "Oh my God, you are really thinking of killing yourself? That sounds terrible! I had no idea that you were on the edge of so much pain that you wanted to end it all! We must go to the emergency room, or I will call 911!"

Suicide Plan: This is a concrete plan including the means and methods to commit suicide. The conditions for when it will occur may be carefully thought out and planned ("If I don't have a job by my thirtieth birthday..."). Or it may be a completely impulsive action without forethought regarding the timing ("I just can't take it anymore"). If a family member knows the means to the plan (like pills, knife, razor, or rope), it's advisable to remove these means from the house, lock them away, and keep an eye out if they are being smuggled into the house. Have an open conversation with your loved one about what your response will be if such means are found.

Suicide Attempt: An attempted suicide is engaging in life-threatening behavior to end one's life. Intention is what defines a suicide attempt, including both clear and ambivalent intention.

Lethal Means: If your loved one is at risk of suicide and you have already removed the means that they consider using, there are additional things to remove from the house: guns, lethal doses of medications, and more than a small amount of alcohol.

If you have any guns in your house and a family member is at risk of suicide, it's important to remove them from the premises! A gun is a lethal weapon that can be used impulsively. Most other forms of suicide are less deadly and require more time to act out. Those few minutes may save a life by creating time for a person to change their mind, ask for help, or just get frustrated and give up. Do not kid yourself that your adult kids or distant relatives cannot find the guns, ammunition, and keys to the gun rack. No guns in the house can be the difference between the life and death of your suicidal loved one.

Medications: Don't keep lethal doses at home. Your doctor, pharmacist, or the poison control center (in the United States: 1-800-222-1222) may be able to help you determine safe quantities for the medicines you need. Be particularly aware of keeping opiate painkillers and benzodiazepines under lock and key, both because of their lethality and their potential for abuse.

Alcohol: Alcohol abuse makes recovery from underlying mental health disorders much more difficult and increases the likelihood of suicide attempts. Alcohol increases the lethality of a drug overdose. Keep only small quantities at home. If your loved one consumes alcohol excessively, you may need to communicate and enforce no alcohol in your house (see chapter 9 for help with this conversation).

Talking About Suicide and Self-Harm

In the heat of emotional dysregulation, when self-harming ideation, threats, or plans are on the table, first manage your own emotions. If someone is in a crisis and considering suicide or self-injury, pay attention to their emotion and validate it. A crisis is not the time to focus on historical factors, explanations, blame, or responsibility. Here are tips for how to do this.

1. Do not be afraid of being direct. If there are hints of suicide, name the elephant in the room and ask directly, "Are you having thoughts of suicide?" or "Are you considering ending your life?"

2. Try to identify factors that precipitated the current suicidal feelings. Validate the person's emotional distress as an understandable result of those factors.

3. Do *not* respond with shaming explanations of the suicidal or self-harming behavior.

4. Present suicidal behavior as a response to a problem and an ineffective solution. If possible, accompany the loved one in the search for a solution to the problem that generated the crisis.

5. Talk about all the reasons your loved one has to live, what is important to them, who depends upon them, and who they love. Highlight and strengthen those connections. "I know how much you love your dog, and he loves you. Nobody will take care of him if you're gone." Or "I know how much your nieces would miss you, and you would miss them."

6. Ask if your loved one has a specific suicide plan (how, when, where) and listen without judgment.

7. Evaluate access to lethal methods, including drugs, weapons, knives, razors, poisons, rope, and the like. Pay attention to those methods that your family member would choose to use. Remove them from the house and keep knives, sharp objects, and cleaning solutions locked up.

Accompany them with validation, and guide them to tolerate their painful feelings. Do not exacerbate the situation with panic reactions or criticism. Focus attention on reducing distress and emotional dysregulation or problem-solving and not arguing over the right to die!

Obsessive Suicidal Ideation

Perhaps your loved one talks about suicide frequently. They may describe their right to do it or the benefits of suicide, or they may just make vague references ("You'll be sorry..." or "I won't be around then"). If there is chronic or obsessive suicidal ideation in response to every little problem that arises, consider how you or other family members might be reinforcing this behavior.

If you stop accommodating and reinforcing chronic suicidal ideation, extinction bursts will likely occur. You will have to be prepared to tolerate your fear, intensively validate your loved one's suffering, reinforce behaviors that replace suicidal thinking, organize support from extended family, friends, and professionals, and have a crisis plan in place.

• *Anne and Her Family*

Anne had a history of self-harm, suicidal ideation, and one attempt, often using these threats to get what she wanted from her parents, insisting that some new gift would give her a reason to live. The few times they finally and firmly said no, she checked herself into one of the best private psychiatric hospitals in the region, saying she just wanted to die. Her siblings and cousins visited her. After a week, she felt better and went home.

The family realized they were reinforcing Anne's problem behaviors. They decided to show no interest in suicidal thoughts and instead reinforce the use of distress tolerance skills. They agreed to validate her feelings and insisted she try distress tolerance skills first, before they would pay attention or support her hospitalization.

Anne did not like the new system. She complained, avoided, and blamed everyone for suddenly not caring. She threatened suicide. Every family member she turned to asked her to try a few skills first before they would listen to her. She repeated how the skills didn't help. When she demanded to go to the hospital for her suicidal thoughts, her mother offered to pay for a taxi. She was furious and refused to go. Anne never went to the hospital again for suicidal ideation.

988 Lifeline and 741741 Crisis Text Line

In the United States, the 988 Lifeline provides confidential support for people in distress, considering suicide, or feeling urges to self-harm. Let your loved one know about the possibility of calling 988 and talking to someone anytime if friends or family don't understand or are unavailable. The national hotline is a network of local crisis centers and varies in availability and wait times (be patient if necessary).

The Crisis Text Line has crisis counselors responding to text messages. Text HOME to 741741 from anywhere in the United States or use WhatsApp. International resources can be found at:

- Befrienders Worldwide: https://www.befrienders.org /need-to-talk

- Find a Helpline: https://findahelpline.com (Freedenthal 2023)

These resources are not just for your loved one. You can call or text if you have any questions about how to respond, how to help, or what local resources are available.

Hospital Emergency Room

Many hospitals offer psychiatric emergency services that typically last less than one week. With a few exceptions, it may be where a person is stabilized with sedatives or other medication to reduce the behavioral problems that landed them there.

For some, hospitalizations are experienced as positive and may reinforce the behavior that led up to the ER visit. Hospitalization immediately after suicide attempts can be problematic if it is experienced as warm, loving, or extremely pleasant. If getting out of the house, having room service three times a day, and chatting with kind doctors and nurses is experienced as a vacation, it may increase the probability that the suicidal behavior is repeated. For others, hospitalization may be a traumatic experience that is never forgotten. It should not be such a pleasant experience that it reinforces problem behavior, nor should it result in PTSD.

Hospitalization is not just for the patient. It may be necessary if the family or the outpatient therapy team is exhausted, cannot get relief from unending crises, and need a break. Some hospitals invite family members in for family therapy or connect families with support groups. This can open the door to getting the relief, connections, and support families often need.

Emergency Call

An emergency call should be made if someone says that suicide is their only option. Call 911 or the number for the mobile crisis team if there is one in your area. (To find the emergency number in countries other than the United States, go to: https://travel.state.gov/content/dam /students-abroad/pdfs/911_ABROAD.pdf. Remember, there is no guarantee that the operator will speak your language.)

If you receive a message via text, telephone, or email from someone who says that they are about to kill themselves or have already done so, take it seriously. Anything similar to the text messages that follow would be a reason to call 911 immediately!

- "This text message is goodbye and farewell to my family and friends. As you know, I have been suffering for years. I have decided that it is just too much to keep trying, and I am ending my life. I am at peace with my decision. I love you all."

- "By the time you get this email, I will be dead. You will finally get what you always wanted."

Tell the 911 operator that this suicide attempt has probably occurred and give them the address. Describe the situation to the operator as a mental health crisis. If you know for sure whether guns are present or not, tell the operator. If you are at the site with your loved one, it can be helpful to meet the police or first responders outside the house to explain the situation.

• *Ulrich and Carl*

Ulrich described an incident with his sixteen-year-old son Carl. "I was joking around with Carl, and suddenly, he was furious with me. Yelling at me, he went straight to the bathroom. He locked himself inside, screaming that he was going to kill himself. I could hear him hitting things while I was telling him to unlock the door. I couldn't get the door open and I was panicking. I called the police. When they arrived at the house ten minutes later, he opened the bathroom door, his hair greased back, looking perfect, and the bathroom was clean. He graciously thanked them for coming because he wanted to file a police report of child abuse against me. They actually took me to the police station!"

Mobile Crisis Teams

Police presence may escalate a mental health crisis, or suicide (or homicide) threats, and increase the level of violence, especially if the police are perceived as—or actually are—acting in a way that is threatening and dangerous. Ten percent of all fatal police shootings occur when the police are called to a mental health crisis. If your loved one is a person of color, that risk is greater. A mobile crisis team consists of trained mental health crisis responders.

Learn what resources are available. Some questions to ask: Does the local hospital have a psychiatry department, and how do they handle psychiatric emergencies? (Go and visit them to learn more and see for yourself!) Do they have any mobile crisis teams? Stop into the local police station and ask them if there are any family crisis services for persons with mental health problems. In the United States, you can call 988 to find out more about suicide prevention resources near you or how to respond in an emergency.

◆ *Diane and Sheila*

Diane's daughter, Sheila, had been increasingly depressed. She told her mother repeatedly that she wanted to quit her job. Her two elderly cats were ill. She had no friends. Sheila said, "I can't take it any longer—my life is almost over."

Diane asked, "So what are you thinking of doing?"

Sheila responded, "I am ending my life."

"Honey, how would you do that? Do you have a plan?"

"I'm not going to tell you, but I am done. You can pick up my cats tomorrow. I'm a terrible cat mother anyway."

"Sheila, please tell me that you will keep yourself safe today and tonight."

"No, Mom. I'm not."

"Sheila, if you are planning on ending your life today, I have to call 911."

"If you do that, I will be furious. I will never speak to you again."

"So then, what will you do to keep yourself safe?"

"Nothing. I can't take this anymore, and I can't take you anymore." Then she hung up.

Diane was not certain that Sheila was intent on suicide at that moment, but proposing suicide and refusing help was an untenable position for her. Fortunately, in her municipality, the police had a trained mobile crisis unit that went out to do a mental health check. When they arrived, Sheila insisted that she was fine and had no intention of suicide. However, she was angry with her mother and did not speak to her for several weeks. Over the following months, she brought it up many times as proof of how little her mother really cared because she did nothing but "call the cops." Diane replied each time that she loved her and wanted her to live. Sheila pleaded and threatened her mother to never call 911 again, but Diane calmly and firmly refused to agree.

Develop a Plan for Suicide Prevention

Some adolescents and young adults don't want to self-harm and are open to receiving support from their families. Invite them to jointly write a plan to manage a crisis and prevent self-harm. If your loved one refuses to engage in crisis planning or preventing self-harm, then invite the rest of the family to discuss it together. Put your plan in writing and make sure everyone agrees to it. If you are the only source of connection and support for your loved one, consider getting support from a mental health professional, the suicide hotline at 988, or a friend who is also open to learning about best practices for preventing self-harm.

If your loved one has a history of suicide and it was never discussed, it's okay to ask about it, if you really want. Find a moment that is relatively calm and relaxed, if possible. Ask questions without judgment. What triggered it? How did they get through it? Do they think about it again? Be curious. Look for reasons your loved one had, and has, to live and note them. Assess the current level of risk.

Here are things to consider as you develop a family-based suicide prevention plan.

- Explore ways to resolve or avoid the triggers that lead to thoughts of suicide.

- Help your loved one think about more skillful ways of expressing themselves and asking for help. (For example, instead of calling you at work and saying, "If you don't come over right away, I'll kill myself," help your daughter to say, "I need to talk to you as soon as possible.")

- Identify the resources your loved one can use at the time of crisis. Explore crisis survival and distress tolerance skills, call a professional or a hotline to talk, or engage in other unproblematic distractions.

- If your loved one is reluctant to commit to using skills, find a way to do them together. (For example, bring two glasses of ice water and an ice bucket to "cool down" together, interact with the family pet, go for a walk together, ask your loved one to count ten breaths with you.)

- Determine where you would go for professional help. Is there a mental health professional working with you or your loved one? Is there a mobile crisis unit in your area?

- Brainstorm how your loved one can tolerate the discomfort until help arrives.

- Anticipate any difficulties that may arise with the plan.

In the United States, the 988 Suicide and Crisis Lifeline offers support and information. It can be a resource for you to get more information regarding how to respond, whether to call the police or an ambulance, whether there is a local mobile crisis unit in your area, and how to respond in a way that helps the person stay safe—either in the moment or planning ahead for a possible emergency.

• *Sue and Bruce*

Bruce had suffered emotional ups and downs for many years. He hated the psychiatric medications that his family made him take. One day, his best friend, Sue, asked him if he ever thought about suicide. He told her the truth. He had decided that if he was not feeling better by his next birthday (two months away), he was going to end his life. He already had tested out a place to hang himself and had the rope stashed away.

Sue could not stop thinking about that conversation. The next day, she called 988 to ask what she should do. A suicide counselor coached her on how to tell Bruce's family about his plan and then deal with Bruce's reaction if he got mad at her. The counselor also explained what to do if an emergency was imminent. Bruce's family sent him to a psychiatric hospital. He didn't like it, but he didn't fight it. He understood that he could be hospitalized against his will if he did not sign himself in. Sue visited him regularly in the hospital. He was released after stabilizing on a different set of medications.

exercise: Suicide Prevention Plan

Are you suffering anxiety or other chronic or acute distress regarding your loved one's suicidal ideation? If so, what distress tolerance skills will you regularly practice?

_____

_____

_____

_____

_____

_____

_____

Do you need additional support? What additional support will you seek out to manage your distress (from friends, family, support groups, mental health professionals)?

_____

_____

_____

Are you skillful at validating your loved one's feelings selectively, without reinforcing problem behaviors? Write at least two short validating responses you could use when your loved one is in a crisis or thinking of ending their suffering by ending their life.

_____

_____

_____

What are the reasons that your loved one has to live and build a life worth living? Consider what is going well in their life. What is important to them? What gives their life meaning? What is pleasant or positive or at least not negative? Write these reasons down.

_____

_____

_____

Can you explore other solutions with your loved one that might help them to reduce their suffering more effectively?

_____

_____

_____

_____

What methods would your loved one use if they were to attempt suicide? Are there lethal means you must remove from the house or put under lock and key? When will you do that?

_____

_____

_____

What resources are available in your area, what is the phone number, when can you call, and how does it work? List below the phone numbers for any mobile crisis services, police and ambulance responses to psychiatric emergencies, emergency intake at the hospital, psychiatric hospitals in your area, suicide hotline, and other community mental health organizations and services that may be available.

_____

_____

_____

Do you need to describe (and potentially act upon) a contingency plan? If your loved one says that they want to end their life and they cannot keep themselves safe, then how will you respond? Write out what you will say and do.

_____

_____

_____

_____

_____

_____

_____

Do you plan on communicating what you will say and do to your loved one in advance? What will you say? Use the DEAR MAN format, if that helps. For example:

Describe: Sometimes you say something that suggests you are thinking about ending your life, I get scared.

Express: Ending your life is permanent and nonnegotiable.

Assert: If I ask you whether you can keep yourself safe and you say no, I will call the mobile crisis unit or 988 and request they take whatever steps necessary to ensure you are safe from harm.

Reinforce: My goal is for you to be safe and recover from stress and suffering.

Now, you try it:

_____

_____

_____

_____

_____

_____

_____

You can download this worksheet with the online free tools, so you can be prepared for prevention.

Summary

If your loved one is in an emotional crisis and mentions self-harm or suicide, remain firm, calm, and centered. Practice crisis survival and distress tolerance skills so you can be rock solid regarding your support for life and prevention of death. You can be caring and open to listening without judgment, and you can be closed to negotiating any agreement with the untenable options of suicide or self-harm. Call for support, backup, professional, or emergency help if you need it.

You may do everything to prevent your loved one from attempting suicide, but there is no way to make a suicide attempt impossible. There is no guarantee that it will never happen, although you can respond as effectively as possible. Acceptance of these facts will help you live your life and take care of yourself, validate your loved one, encourage and support their mental health recovery, and call appropriate professional resources when necessary.

CHAPTER 11

Radical Acceptance

Consider the Buddhist parable of the two arrows. If an arrow strikes a person, is it painful? Of course, it is painful. If a second arrow strikes a person, is it more painful? Undoubtedly, being struck by two arrows would be more painful than one.

The first strike may be any of life's slings and arrows over which you have no control. Someone says something judgmental, inconveniences you, or does something you don't like. The first arrow can be any negative experience.

Then you launch the second arrow, as we all do. This is the arrow of resistance to reality. When you shoot the second arrow, it will generate more suffering—yours. You increase and sustain your own misery, believing another person wants to make you angry or blaming yourself for being a pushover. You may be grumbling about how this person should change their behavior, quietly seething with self-righteous indignation, wallowing in hopelessness that things will never change, or even denying that it matters. How often do you get swept up in one of these reactions?

The suffering of the second arrow arises when you refuse to accept the unpleasant situation or cling to thinking about how things are so unfair or unfortunate. The path to freedom from this misery and suffering is letting go of what you urgently want, tolerating the moment as it is, and being willing to experience the discomfort of your emotional response. This is radical acceptance.

Resistance Separates

Tenacity, persistence, striving, and control are all useful and desirable. Our social system applauds and rewards such characteristics in education, work, sports, and all types of performance. All of these qualities come together into what we might describe as "grit," and we all need it! You may have important achievements thanks to your grit.

Yet too much of a good thing can end up being dysfunctional. An excess of tenacity and persistence is tense, rigid, and insistent. Too much effort and striving can be an exhausting struggle. When grit becomes excessive, we might call it stubbornness, over-control, or resistance to reality.

Resistance has many faces. It can look like a temper tantrum, giving up and standing idly by when action is required, over-controlling instruction, or compulsively solving problems. "Do it this way" or "I can fix it for you." Resistance impairs cooperation, growth, change, and problem-solving. Resistance separates people from each other.

Acceptance Connects

Imagine giving your loved one the freedom to be just as they are in the present moment, fully accepting all their patterns of thinking, speaking, and acting. This is a practice of accepting their motivations, humanness, and foibles.

While you are at it, try giving yourself the freedom to be just as you are—independent of the need to be understood or liked. It's okay to want to help a loved one, but you will likely be a lot more effective if you can first pause to see exactly what's happening with patience and acceptance. It may be one minute, one hour, one day, or one week. It's highly likely to result in more insight and understanding, which are precursors to more effective change.

• *Angela, Becky, and Charli*

Angela's daughter, Becky, was a mom with emotional dysregulation. Angela's heart ached for her granddaughter, Charli. Becky often criticized Charli for laziness, lack of attention, inadequate grades, poor eating habits, and more. At the tender age of twelve, when her mother ranted, Charli sometimes cried silently or froze with fear and confusion.

Angela learned years ago that she should not comment on her daughter's parenting. Yet Angela couldn't control herself and continued to offer gentle suggestions that invariably backfired. Angela knew that it would be impossible to take Charli away from her mother, and if she tried, Becky would probably cut her off from all contact. She also knew that Becky loved Charli despite her excessive criticism.

Angela felt like she had to practice acceptance of her daughter's behavior twenty times a day sometimes, but it paid off. The more she practiced acceptance of her daughter's unstable parenting and validated how hard it was to be a mother, the more space Angela had to be a consistent and validating presence in her granddaughter's life.

What Acceptance Is Not

Don't confuse acceptance with other concepts that are deceptively similar, but upon closer consideration, are quite different.

Approval: One does not have to approve of something to allow it to be as it is. Approval implies a value judgment: "Yes, that is good; I approve." Acceptance allows reality to be just as it is in the present moment.

Indifference: Indifference is a lack of interest or concern that moves you away from acceptance and disconnects you from reality.

Unchangeable: Acceptance recognizes that things will change in the future. You can hope your loved one moves toward recovery and also accept that they currently have chronic mental health issues and may not be interested in recovery today.

Resignation: Unlike acts of resignation or passivity, acceptance opens your attention to the experience and makes you aware of your feelings about the situation, even when it is aversive. Acceptance is an active presence.

Radical acceptance is an active choice. You will find many opportunities to make this hard choice and practice acceptance. Something painful occurs, and there you are, one more time, about to launch the second arrow. You may resist, complain, fix, push away, ignore the situation, and increase your misery in countless ways. Every mistake you make is an opportunity to practice acceptance again!

exercise: Half Smile and Willing Hands

Identify something you need to accept. Describe it in words free of value judgments. Just the facts. Once you decide exactly what you need to accept, let it go for a few minutes and follow these instructions.

Sit in a comfortable position, hands on your lap, palms up, or lie down with hands at your sides, palms up. These are Willing Hands, open to accepting reality just as it is.

Relax your face from the tip of your head to your chin and jaw. Imagine your forehead expanding. Notice sensations in the eyelids and the fine muscles around the eyes. Feel the sensations in the cheeks. Notice sensations in the lips—the skin of the lips and the muscles. Move the attention to the interior of the mouth, the tongue, and the throat. Separate the teeth, let go of tension in the jaw, and feel the chin's weight.

With your face relaxed, imagine the cheeks floating upward toward the eyes and gently lifting the corners of the mouth. This is a subtle Half Smile, a serene facial expression that is not necessarily visible to others. It sends information from behind your face to your brain that you are calm, serene, and accepting.

Now remember the words that describe the reality you need to accept. With a Half Smile and Willing Hands, gently repeat these words several times with a relaxed and casual tone of voice that communicates total acceptance.

Accepting the Unexpected

Life may not have unfolded as you expected. Your family relationships, the behaviors of an emotionally dysregulated loved one, and the accommodations that you make for your loved one are probably nothing like what you imagined. Consider Corrine's experience as a metaphor.

◆ *Corrine*

I wanted to live in France for most of my life. I studied French in high school and college. I dreamed of sipping café au lait there, taking art classes in Paris, skiing in the French Alps in the winters, and spending summers in the French Riviera. I even visited Paris twice!

I worked for decades to save money to move to France, but it was much harder than expected. Then someone told me that Buenos Aires is the "Paris of South America," and living there was far more affordable than in France.

Argentina? That was not my plan. They don't even speak French! However, I realized that obtaining a visa and living in Paris was beyond my reach. I sold my house and car and found myself in Buenos Aires, alone, more scared than I had imagined, and unable to speak the language.

When I got to know Argentina, I learned that Buenos Aires has delightful cafes, beautiful urban parks, and French-inspired architecture. Patagonia's remote natural beauty hosts iconic wildlife. I spent fifteen years there and learned to speak fluent Castellano, their beautiful version of Spanish.

I had a close friend in France who told me about her life there. Her friends were culturally sophisticated artists and writers, and the cuisine was extraordinary. When I told her about the free museums and the barbecued steaks, she was either silent or expressed her judgments about Latin America. My friends back home in the States never understood why I moved to Argentina.

I will never be a resident of France, study art in Paris, or ski in the Alps. But I strolled along Rio de la Plata every day, drank the ubiquitous mate with friends, and danced tango in the milongas of Buenos Aires several times a week. I speak fluent Spanish now.

Your former hopes, plans, and expectations may differ greatly from your life today. Your friends and family may not understand your situation and even give you bad advice or blame you for it. Like a stranger in a strange land, it can feel lonely, confusing, and even scary. Don't shoot the second arrow of resistance and add to your pain.

exercise: Accepting Your Family Life

Reflecting upon this story, write down some unexpected and undesired things in your life. Be specific and eliminate judgmental language. Remember, you do not have to accept anything about the future. Acceptance of reality is allowing the present to be as it is and the past to be as it was.

_____

_____

_____

_____

For each fact or situation that you need to accept, rank your current level of acceptance at this moment according to the following scale.

0   Aversion—Avoiding, denying, or ignoring the issue or situation.

1   Touch and go—Barely any contact with the situation.

2   Curiosity—Being aware of the emotions and reactions that the situation generates.

3   Tolerance—Permitting yourself to be in contact with the situation in a more stable way.

4   Openness—Allowing things to be as they are and holding space for the emotions.

5   Radical Acceptance—Fully accepting the situation, being at peace, and seeing the hidden value. (The "hidden value" may be something new or positive, although it does not override the pain.)

Select one example from your list to practice accepting. Check to ensure you are focused on accepting only facts, not evaluations, and only in the present or the past.

Level of acceptance before completing the practice (0 to 5): _____

Now, read the following list and try them with your selected example.

- Repeat what you must accept in a voice that communicates acceptance and conviction.

- Pay attention to physical body sensations when considering what you have to accept.

- Imagine what you would do if the facts you are trying to accept were true.

- Allow your mind to be open to all the consequences of this reality.

- Allow yourself to experience disappointment, sadness, or grief around the situation.

- Practice a Half Smile and Willing Hands as you imagine yourself accepting what you need to accept.

- Imagine what you would do if you had already accepted it.

Level of acceptance after completing the practice (0 to 5): _____

Describe your experiences, the effectiveness of the practice, and any new insights.

_____

_____

_____

_____

_____

_____

_____

Summary

Radical acceptance is a path to well-being, satisfaction, and happiness. It improves relationships, connects people with each other, and relieves suffering. It's not passive. It is a very active practice of accepting what unfolds and knowing that life is ever-changing. With eyes open and palms upward, you are present and accepting, ready to meet the world and receive what the universe delivers each day. When a situation changes, you will be present and able to respond more effectively.

CHAPTER 12

Final Words

Dialectics is a panoramic philosophy that helps you recognize that acceptance and change are integrated as you struggle to resolve problems, find gratitude for what you have, and move through life. You are doing your best to clean up your side of the street in this relationship, and it is also true that you can do better. Just like your loved one.

As you reach the end of this workbook, take a few minutes to mindfully sit still and quiet. Then read the following ten vows aloud and listen to your own words.

I vow to...

1. Be more present and aware of my emotional state, even when it is unpleasant.

2. Be mindful and self-compassionate when judgments, criticism, interpretations, or stubbornness arise.

3. Improve my communication and the quality of my relationships by listening more, observing with greater attention, and accurately reflecting back what others say to me.

4. Validate the emotions of others, even when they seem excessive or confusing to me.

5. Positively reinforce the effective and desired behavior of my loved ones.

6. Avoid giving advice and ask more questions.

7. Avoid trying to solve other people's problems and instead accompany them in their search for solutions only when they ask me to.

8. Take responsibility for practicing tender and fierce self-compassion to observe and protect my limits with kindness and compassion toward others.

9. Practice radical acceptance of my life and the things about others that I cannot change, even when it is frustrating or disappointing.

10. Guide my behavior by the need to be effective instead of the need to be right.

Sustain your new skills! Choose one vow each week and find concrete ways to practice it throughout the week. In ten weeks, your family life will have shifted for the better.

References

American Psychiatric Association (APA). 2016. *Desk Reference to the Diagnostic Criteria from DSM-5*. Arlington, VA: APA.

Andrewes, H. E., C. Hulbert, S. M. Cotton, J. Betts, and A. M. Chanen. 2019. "Relationships Between the Frequency and Severity of Non-Suicidal Self-Injury and Suicide Attempts in Youth with Borderline Personality Disorder." *Early Intervention Psychiatry* 13: 194–201.

Bernanos, G. 2002. *The Diary of a Country Priest*. Cambridge, MA: Da Capo Press.

Biskin, R. S., and J. Paris. 2013. "Comorbidities in Borderline Personality Disorder." *Psychiatric Times* 30(1).

Carey, B. 2011. "Expert on Mental Illness Reveals Her Own Fight." *New York Times*, June 23. https://www.nytimes.com/2011/06/23/health/23lives.html.

Duschinsky, R., and S. Foster. 2021. "Adaptation and Mental Health." *Mentalizing and Epistemic Trust: The Work of Peter Fonagy and Colleagues at the Anna Freud Centre*. New York: Oxford University Press.

Ekman, P. 2007. *Emotions Revealed: Recognizing Faces and Feelings to Improve Communication and Emotional Life*. New York: Holt.

Freedenthal, S. 2023. *Loving Someone with Suicidal Thoughts: What Family, Friends, and Partners Can Say and Do*. Oakland, CA: New Harbinger Publications.

Fruzzetti, A. E. 2006. *The High-Conflict Couple: A Dialectical Behavior Therapy Guide to Finding Peace, Intimacy, and Validation*. Oakland, CA: New Harbinger Publications.

Grant, B. F., S. P. Chou, R. B. Goldstein, B. Huang, F. S. Stinson, T. D. Saha, S. M. Smith, et al. 2008. "Prevalence, Correlates, Disability, and Comorbidity of DSM-IV Borderline Personality Disorder: Results from the Wave 2 National Epidemiologic Survey on Alcohol and Related Conditions." *The Journal of Clinical Psychiatry* 69(4): 533–545.

Linehan, M. M. 1993. *Cognitive Behavioral Treatment of Borderline Personality Disorder.* New York: Guilford Press.

———. 2015. *DBT Skills Training Handouts and Worksheets,* 2nd ed. New York: Guilford Press.

———. 2020. *Building a Life Worth Living: A Memoir.* New York: Random House.

Linehan, M. M., S. Rizvi, S. Shaw-Welch, and B. Page. 2008. "Psychiatric Aspects of Suicidal Behaviour: Personality Disorders." In *The International Handbook of Suicide and Attempted Suicide,* edited by K. Hawton and K. van Heeringen. Hoboken, NJ: John Wiley & Sons.

Lundberg, G., and J. Lundberg. 1995. *I Don't Have to Make Everything All Better: Six Practical Principles That Empower Others to Solve Their Own Problems While Enriching Your Relationship.* New York: Penguin Books.

Lynch, T. R. 2018. *Radically Open Dialectical Behavior Therapy: Theory and Practice for Treating Disorders of Overcontrol.* Oakland, CA: New Harbinger Publications.

Manning, S. Y. 2011. *Loving Someone with Borderline Personality Disorder: How to Keep Out-of-Control Emotions from Destroying Your Relationship.* New York: Guilford Press.

Miller, A. L., J. H. Rathus, and M. M. Linehan. 2007. *Dialectical Behavior Therapy with Suicidal Adolescents.* New York: Guilford Press.

Neff, K. D. 2021. *Fierce Self-Compassion: How Women Can Harness Kindness to Speak Up, Claim Their Power, and Thrive.* New York: HarperCollins.

Raes, F., E. Pommier, K. D. Neff, and D. Van Gucht. 2011. "Construction and Factorial Validation of a Short Form of the Self-Compassion Scale." *Clinical Psychology & Psychotherapy* 18: 250–255.

Siegel, D. S. 2022. *Intraconnected: MWe (Me + We) as the Integration of Self, Identity, and Belonging.* New York: W. W. Norton.

Taylor, J. B. 2008. *My Stroke of Insight: A Brain Scientist's Personal Journey.* New York: Penguin Books.

Temes, C. M., F. R. Frankenburg, G. M. Fitzmaurice, and M. C. Zanarini. 2019. "Deaths by Suicide and Other Causes Among Patients with Borderline Personality Disorder and Personality-Disordered Comparison Subjects Over 24 Years of Prospective Follow-Up." *Journal of Clinical Psychiatry* 80(1): 18m12436.

TIME. 2018. "Great Scientists: The Geniuses and Visionaries Who Transformed Our World." *TIME*, Special Issue, April 27.

Trull, T. J., L. K. Freeman, T. J. Vebares, A. M. Choate, A. C. Helle, and A. M. Wycoff. 2018. "Borderline Personality Disorder and Substance Use Disorders: An Updated Review." *Borderline Personality Disorder and Emotional Dysregulation* 5: 15.

van der Kolk, B. A. 2014. *The Body Keeps the Score: Brain, Mind, and Body in the Healing of Trauma*. New York: Viking.

Wampold, B. E., and Z. E. Imel. 2015. *The Great Psychotherapy Debate: The Evidence for What Makes Psychotherapy Work*, 2nd ed. New York: Routledge/Taylor & Francis.

World Health Organization (WHO). 2021. *ICD-11: International Classification of Diseases*, 11th rev. Geneva: WHO.

Young, S. 2016. *The Science of Enlightenment: How Meditation Works*. Boulder, CO: Sounds True.

Zanarini, M. C., C. M. Temes, F. R. Frankenburg, D. B. Reich, and G. M. Fitzmaurice. 2018. "Description and Prediction of Time-to-Attainment of Excellent Recovery for Borderline Patients Followed Prospectively for 20 Years." *Psychiatry Research* 262: 40–45.

Corrine Stoewsand, PhD, coaches families on how to manage their relationships and communicate more effectively with loved ones who have symptoms of borderline personality disorder (BPD). She has been leading dialectical behavior therapy (DBT) and mindfulness workshops for families and psychologists internationally since 2006. Stoewsand has had intensive training in DBT from Behavioral Tech Institute, and advanced DBT training from Marsha Linehan. She served as a founding member of Fundación Foro, Buenos Aires, Argentina—the largest and most active DBT team in South America—and then created www.dbtcoach.com to provide online educational programs for families worldwide.

Randi Kreger has brought the concerns of family members who have a loved one with BPD to an international forefront through her website, www.bpdcentral.com, and the Welcome to Oz online support community. Through Eggshells Press, she offers family members a wide variety of specialized booklets and other materials. She was also instrumental in the formation of the Personality Disorders Awareness Network (PDAN), a nonprofit organization. Kreger is author of *Stop Walking on Eggshells*, *The Stop Walking on Eggshells Workbook*, and *The Essential Family Member Guide to Borderline Personality Disorder*, among others. She speaks and gives workshops about BPD internationally.

Carola Pechon is a licensed clinical psychologist in Bariloche, Argentina. She is founder and director of Tandem Asistencia y Formación en Psicoterapia. She is currently a DBT mentor at Behavioral Tech Institute. Pechon has been training mental health professionals in DBT in South America since 2012, and leads a clinical team of psychologists treating children, adolescents, and adults. Learn more at www.tandempsicoterapia.com.ar.

Foreword writer **Anthony P. DuBose, PsyD**, has trained healthcare providers worldwide in the treatment of BPD, substance use disorders, and suicidal and self-injurious behaviors. He is a member of the International Dissemination Committee and the Training Committee of the World Dialectical Behavior Therapy Association (WDBTA), and serves on the WDBTA transitional board of directors as its treasurer.

Real change *is* possible

For more than fifty years, New Harbinger has published
proven-effective self-help books and pioneering
workbooks to help readers of all ages and backgrounds
improve mental health and well-being, and achieve lasting
personal growth. In addition, our spirituality books
offer profound guidance for deepening awareness and
cultivating healing, self-discovery, and fulfillment.

Founded by psychologist Matthew McKay and
Patrick Fanning, New Harbinger is proud to be
an independent, employee-owned company.
Our books reflect our core values of integrity, innovation,
commitment, sustainability, compassion, and trust.
Written by leaders in the field and recommended by
therapists worldwide, New Harbinger books are practical,
accessible, and provide real tools for real change.

 **newharbinger**publications

More Books

This self-help classic will show you how to stand up for yourself and assert your needs, defuse arguments and conflicts, and bring peace and stability back into your life.

978-1684036899 / US $20.95

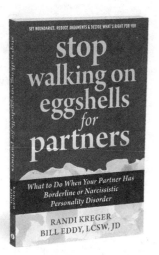

If your partner has BPD or NPD, this book will help you evaluate your relationship, identify your own needs, set limits, and reclaim your sense of self.

978-1608824878 / US $19.95

This essential guide offers powerful skills for navigating your child's disorder—without compromising your family or yourself.

978-1684038510 / US $20.95

A roadmap for anyone divorcing a high-conflict person. This book will help you navigate the legal, psychological, and emotional aspects of divorce so you can stay empowered.

978-1684036110 / US $21.95

new harbinger publications

1-800-748-6273 / newharbinger.com

Did you know there are **free tools** you can download for this book?

Free tools are things like **worksheets**, **guided meditation exercises**, and **more** that will help you get the most out of your book.

You can download free tools for this book— whether you bought or borrowed it, in any format, from any source—from the New Harbinger website. All you need is a NewHarbinger.com account. Just use the URL provided in this book to view the free tools that are available for it. Then, click on the "download" button for the free tool you want, and follow the prompts that appear to log in to your NewHarbinger.com account and download the material.

You can also save the free tools for this book to your **Free Tools Library** so you can access them again anytime, just by logging in to your account! Just look for this button on the book's free tools page. ➤

+ Save this to my free tools library

If you need help accessing or downloading free tools, visit **newharbinger.com/faq** or contact us at **customerservice@newharbinger.com.**